AN A–Z OF JANE AUSTEN

AN A–Z OF JANE AUSTEN

Michael Greaney

BLOOMSBURY ACADEMIC
LONDON • NEW YORK • OXFORD • NEW DELHI • SYDNEY

BLOOMSBURY ACADEMIC
Bloomsbury Publishing Plc
50 Bedford Square, London, WC1B 3DP, UK
1385 Broadway, New York, NY 10018, USA
29 Earlsfort Terrace, Dublin 2, Ireland

BLOOMSBURY, BLOOMSBURY ACADEMIC and the Diana logo
are trademarks of Bloomsbury Publishing Plc

First published in Great Britain 2023
Copyright © Michael Greaney, 2023

Michael Greaney has asserted his right under the Copyright, Designs and
Patents Act, 1988, to be identified as Author of this work.

For legal purposes the Acknowledgements on p. vii constitute
an extension of this copyright page.

Cover design and illustration by Rebecca Heselton

Bloomsbury Publishing Plc does not have any control over, or responsibility for, any
third-party websites referred to or in this book. All internet addresses given in this
book were correct at the time of going to press. The author and publisher regret
any inconvenience caused if addresses have changed or sites have ceased
to exist, but can accept no responsibility for any such changes.

A catalogue record for this book is available from the British Library.

A catalog record for this book is available from the Library of Congress.

ISBN: HB: 978-1-3502-5421-3
        PB: 978-1-3502-5420-6
        ePDF: 978-1-3502-5424-4
        eBook: 978-1-3502-5423-7

Typeset by Integra Software Services Pvt. Ltd.
Printed and bound in India

To find out more about our authors and books visit www.bloomsbury.com
and sign up for our newsletters.

CONTENTS

Contents

ACKNOWLEDGEMENTS

This book has its origins in undergraduate modules on Austen that I have taught at Lancaster University, and I would like to thank our students for teaching me so much about her work.

I would also like to thank Lucy Alcock, Arthur Bradley, Jo Carruthers, Matthew Dunlop, Harriet Newnes, Michaela Robinson-Tate and Andrew Tate for their generous support, encouragement and feedback as I was working on this book.

TEXTS AND ABBREVIATIONS

Quotations from Austen's fiction are taken from the Cambridge edition. Quotations from her letters are from the Oxford University Press edition (4th edition), edited by Deirdre Le Faye.

E = Emma
J = Juvenilia
L = Letters
LM = Later Manuscripts
MP = Mansfield Park
NA = Northanger Abbey
P = Persuasion
PP = Pride and Prejudice
SS = Sense and Sensibility

INTRODUCTION

This book is an exploratory guide to the writings of **Jane** Austen. Organized alphabetically, it contains a series of interconnected discussions of twenty-six keywords taken from those writings, from **accident** to **zigzag**. These include places (**Bath, West Indies**), things (**eye, horse, letter**), concepts (**kindness, queer, risk**), activities and practices (**dance, matchmaking, visit**), and categories of personhood (**children, friend, servant**). Covered here are Austen's six full-length novels from *Northanger Abbey* to *Persuasion* but the analysis also extends to her letters, unfinished novels and teenage writings, and to lesser-known items such as her prayers and her marginalia. Using Austen's own words to explore her writings from the inside out, this book aims to achieve fresh and stimulating perspectives on the work of one of the most celebrated authors in literary history.

Jane Austen was born in 1775 in Steventon, Hampshire, the seventh of the eight children of George and Cassandra Austen. Apart from a five-year spell in Bath, she lived most of her life in the county of her birth. She didn't go to university, or get married, or have children, or travel the world or interact with other major writers of her day. Commenting on her relative isolation from influential literary circles, her nephew James Edward Austen-Leigh calls her a 'home-made' writer (2002: 90). Austen wrote from an early age to entertain herself and her family and to flex her prodigious literary talent, and she went on to publish four novels in her lifetime: *Sense and Sensibility* (1811), *Pride and Prejudice* (1813), *Mansfield Park* (1814) and *Emma* (1815); shortly after her death, two further novels appeared under titles chosen by her family: *Northanger Abbey* and *Persuasion* (both 1817). But the totality of her literary achievement does not end with these six novels. The Austen corpus has been significantly extended and enriched as previously unpublished manuscript material has entered the public domain and attracted critical attention. There are numerous short dramas, parodies, skits and epistolary narratives written during her teenage years, a body of work including texts such as 'Lesley Castle' and 'Love and Freindship' [*sic*] whose flair and gleeful inventiveness is winning increasing critical recognition (see Johnston 2021). There is *Lady Susan*, written in the 1790s, a compact epistolary novel about coquetry as a way of life (confusingly, Whit Stillman's 2016 film adaptation of this text was entitled *Love & Friendship*). There are also two unfinished novels: *The Watsons*, a melancholy comedy of homecoming, which Austen abandoned in 1805; and *Sanditon*, a bracing seaside satire which was left unfinished when she died. Finally, Austen's letters, though never as richly confessional as we'd want them to be, deserve notice as a record of the minutiae of her daily life that contains tantalizing flashes of insight into her views on the craft of fiction. No one knows how many letters Austen wrote in her lifetime – a well-informed commentator suggests that the number could be anywhere between 2000 and 7000 (Van Ostade 2014: 35) – but only 160 or so survive, the majority of which are to her sister Cassandra (1773–1845), always her most intimate confidante. It was Cassandra who, shortly before her own death, destroyed hundreds of Jane's more personal or revealing letters in order to safeguard her family's privacy and dignity. We will never retrieve the entirety of Austen's writerly output, but the present study seeks to engage with the full range of her writings as they are now available to us.

The novels that Austen published during her lifetime enjoyed decent but by no means runaway sales and received some discerning and appreciative reviews. A private rather than actively secretive writer, Austen published her work anonymously but as it found a readership details of the author's identity soon began to circulate. Her most illustrious admirer was the Prince Regent, the future George IV, who was reported to have a set of her works in each of his residences. Via his librarian, he invited Austen to dedicate a novel to him and when *Emma* was published in December 1815 she obliged with all the appearance of good grace. When Austen died in 1817 her lifetime earnings as an author had amounted to a little less than £700 – a respectable sum, if a long way short of the kind of income that would have made her financially independent. It would be hard to put a figure to the value of the Austen industry since then.

If you want to know more about Austen's life, and how Jane Austen the historical person became Jane Austen the world-famous author, you can turn to **J is for Jane** and start this book there. Or you can start anywhere you like. Unlike most critical studies, this work is not a one-way journey towards a singular argumentative payoff. The structure of this book invites browsing, cross-referencing and lateral thinking. Its twenty-six keywords appear in bold so that readers can plot their own itinerary, one that might take them from, say, **theatre** to Bath to **illness** and so on. But why *these* twenty-six words? The justification for my choices must lie in the analysis I've provided in individual entries, and whatever my preliminary rationale might be no one will find it difficult to imagine an alternative version of this book – one in which, say, C would be for 'charm', or M for 'manner', or W for 'waiting'. And that's all to the good. This book looks intently at a selection of Austen's words but not because its choices represent the last word on Austen.

In its immersive, eye-to-text attention to Austen's way with words, this book takes some inspiration from Stuart Tave's *Some Words of Jane Austen* (1973), a subtle and searching discussion which provides one of the most sympathetically nuanced critical readings that the author has ever received. One point of difference, however, is that Tave's preference is for the abstract end of Austen's vocabulary. His analysis dwells, in rich and rewarding ways, on terms such as *affection, delicacy, elegance, exertion* and *imagination* as they operate in Austen's writings. Like Tave, the present study considers some abstract concepts (kindness, **unexpected**) but it also places significant emphasis on the three-dimensional contents of Austen's worlds (**gift**, letter, theatre), and indeed on words that might not seem immediately classifiable as themes *or* as objects (**no**, zigzag).

Much of this book pays attention to what you might call the 'surface' of Austen's writings – to activities such as dance or matchmaking, for example, whose centrality in her storylines might seem to go without saying. In so doing I'm making the case that readings of Austen don't necessarily have to be esoteric to be fresh or revealing. Some of the major contributions to Austen studies in recent years have focused on the 'secret' or 'hidden' dimensions of her writings. Titles such as D. A. Miller's *Jane Austen, or the Secret of Style* (2003) or John Wiltshire's *The Hidden Jane Austen* (2014) have a certain frisson because they seem to promise access to regions of her fiction that might not otherwise be visible to the naked eye. Inspired by such promises, a reader might approach Austen's writings in the same way that Catherine Morland approaches Northanger Abbey – that is, poised and primed to make thrilling discoveries of secret material buried in the bowels of the text. Nor do Austen's writings, many of which exhibit a fascination with riddles and secrets, always discourage such an approach. But let's not forget, when we read Austen, to attend to what's there in front of us on the surface. Her novels are, in very obvious ways, about social visits, making friends, writing letters and being **young** – but the fact that these experiences are right there on the surface doesn't make them uncomplicated or negligible. Part of the pleasure and challenge of Austen is that the more you read her work, the harder it becomes to say with any confidence what's inconsequentially superficial and what's rewardingly 'deep', what counts as foreground and what lies in the background, what occupies centre-stage and what languishes on the margins. When Austen directs her readers' attention, she engages in all kinds of double-bluff about the trivial and the consequential elements of her fictional worlds. One of her specialities is entrusting potentially fascinating topics to bores, windbags and other ignorable talkers. No one's ears prick up when John Thorpe in *Northanger Abbey* rattles on about horses. But if we do pay attention to horses in Austen – in *Northanger Abbey* and elsewhere – they will enable us to see how equestrian culture sheds light on matters of status, power, gender and mobility in her world. Mr Woodhouse in *Emma* talks about horses too, in his amiably distracted way, and about illness and servants. He doesn't have anything particularly compelling to say on these issues. But Austen does.

The alphabetical structure of this book ties it closely to Austen's own vocabulary. In particular, it takes its cue from Austen's own fondness for games with words and letters. A short poem of 1811, inspired by news reports of the marriage of a 'Mr Gell' of Eastbourne to a 'Miss Gill' of Hackney, revolves delightedly around the one-letter difference between Gill and Gell. The Jane Austen's House Museum at Chawton in Hampshire holds a box of ivory letters once owned by the author that were used for word games. Riddles and games of anagrams feature in *Emma* in ways that become even more conspicuously significant when we re-read the novel. Austen is a professional author who sees no distinction between working with words and playing with them. One of her final pieces of writing is a letter to one of her nieces in which every word is spelled backwards, with six as **xis** and so forth. When Austen looks at the alphabet, the possibilities for pleasurable experiments with words and meaning dance before her eyes. Not all of her characters are quite so eagerly responsive to the imaginative and creative possibilities harboured by those twenty-six letters. In *Mansfield Park*, when the bookish Fanny Price returns to Portsmouth she is disappointed to learn that her rambunctious sister Betsey regards the alphabet as 'her greatest enemy' (*MP*: 453). This book, with all due respect to Betsey, operates on the assumption that the alphabet can be a powerful creative ally in our reading of Austen.

A IS FOR ACCIDENT

The world of **Jane** Austen's fiction is normally a pretty safe place to be, unless you are a character in her teenage writings, in which case the hazards are plentiful and hair-raising. Lucy in 'Jack and Alice' has her leg broken by a steel trap. Henry Hervey in 'Lesley Castle' is thrown from his **horse**, fractures his skull and dies soon after. The action of 'Evelyn' includes a shipwreck with much loss of life in the Solent. The heroines of 'Love and Freindship' witness the death of their husbands in a carriage accident. The vicissitudes of love and fate are experienced, in these early writings, as random physical shocks and collisions that Austen narrates with a gleeful off-handedness that would be unthinkable in the works of her maturity.

Things seem altogether safer in Austen's full-length novels, from *Northanger Abbey* to *Persuasion*, where the more common hazards are psychological rather than physical – the social humiliation of being snubbed at a **dance**, for example, or the frustration of missing out on a fun social event. But even in her mature fiction, physical accidents continue to happen, albeit in less obviously brutal and deadly ways (see Hamilton 2008: 391–410). Whereas the carriage accident in 'Love and Freindship' is a veritable bloodbath, the one that opens her final, unfinished novel, *Sanditon*, is a tamer affair – our hero, Thomas Parker, escapes with a sprained ankle. Even so, physical accidents carry more impact in these later works precisely because they are used more sparingly and with more artful restraint than in her knockabout juvenilia. Consider, in this regard, the moment in *Sense and Sensibility* when a pin in Lady Middleton's headdress grazes her three-year-old daughter's neck (*SS*: 140). It's only a scratch, a tiny pinprick of detail in a rich and complex text, but one that invites interpretation. Can we be sure that this scratch was entirely accidental? Such a question becomes askable by readers influenced by modern psychoanalytic theory. Sigmund Freud ([1901] 2002) influentially argues that 'accidents' are never simply or purely random, and that they can be read as expressions of unconscious desire. Someone who 'involuntarily' breaks a fragile ornament may have had unconscious reasons for doing so. A post-Freudian reader might wonder if Lady Middleton, a seemingly doting mother, harbours a streak of unconscious cruelty towards her child – or even if this episode might be symptomatic of Austen's own imperfectly disguised hostility to **children**.

Involuntary mishaps such as the incident with Lady Middleton's hairpin plunge Austen's fiction into the murky territory of accidentally-on-purpose behaviour. Nowhere are questions of purpose, responsibility and blame more tantalizingly blurred than in the case of Louisa Musgrove's notorious and near-fatal fall from the Cobb at Lyme Regis in *Persuasion*:

> [A]ll were contented to pass quietly and carefully down the steep flight, excepting Louisa; she must be jumped down them by Captain Wentworth. In all their walks, he had had to jump her from the stiles; the sensation was delightful to her. The hardness of the pavement for her feet, made him less willing upon the present occasion; he did it, however; she was safely down, and instantly, to shew her enjoyment, ran up the steps to be jumped down again. He advised her against it, thought the jar too great; but no, he reasoned and talked in vain; she smiled and said, 'I am determined I will:' he put out his hands; she was too precipitate by half a second, she fell on the pavement on the Lower Cobb, and was taken up lifeless!
>
> (*P*: 118)

What makes the scene shocking is the brutal suddenness of its transition from light-hearted play to life-or-death crisis. One moment Louisa is flirting with Captain Wentworth, the next their playful rapport is broken, their bodies are desynchronized and she is seemingly lifeless on the ground. The accident is a medical emergency – one in which Anne Elliot will take charge with swift and unflappable practicality, as though seizing the moment to (re-)establish herself as the protagonist of a novel in which she has been routinely upstaged by her less reticent peers. But once the immediate danger is over, the questions of desire, intention and responsibility that the accident provokes remain unanswered. Do we blame Louisa for recklessly mistiming her jump? Might she, consciously or otherwise, have *wanted* to miss Wentworth's outstretched hands? It certainly seems as though Louisa has used her fall to enact and pre-empt the plunge in narrative status that the novel has in store for her, from the glamorous role of potentially significant love interest to the status of peripheral and effectively voiceless secondary character. On the other hand, is Wentworth at fault for carelessly mistiming his catch – or has he perfectly timed a deliberately unsuccessful catch? Perhaps what we have witnessed here is Wentworth accidentally-on-purpose 'dropping' Louisa because his interest in their game, and indeed their flirtation, has run its course.

Louisa's accident is shockingly **unexpected**, though as we re-read it, we begin to realize that we should have seen it coming. It has been prefigured, for example, in the accident that befalls little Charles Musgrove, who dislocates his collar bone earlier in the novel. It has been prefigured, also, by Louisa's own buoyant excitement in jumping down from stiles in the countryside. And, if we glance back through Austen's work, we will see that it is only one of many significance plunges and tumbles in the pages of her fiction. From Marianne Dashwood losing her footing as she canters downhill (*SS*: 50) to Tom Bertram falling from his **horse** at Newmarket (*MP*: 494) to **Jane** Fairfax nearly tumbling overboard during a Weymouth water-party (*E*: 235), Austen's novels, as one reader has put it, are 'littered with fallen bodies' (Markovits 2007: 779).

Accidental falls in Austen have multiple narrative, symbolic and ethical functions. In narrative terms, they function as beginnings and endings. They can represent an outbreak of new narrative possibilities (romance between Marianne and Willoughby) or a peremptory closing down of old ones (Louisa's accident spells the end of her romantic prospects with Wentworth). They disclose or confirm the precarity of Austen's female characters, showing that it wouldn't take much to tip them over the edge or plunge them into medical, moral or socio-economic crisis. In terms of ethical symbolism, they expose the limits of what is foreseeable and controllable in human life, the ways in which our decisions and desires may be opaque even to ourselves, and – in their jarring impact – they can function as (self-inflicted) punishments for characters whose wayward behaviour is deemed to be in need of sharp correction.

These multiple functions of accident are all visible in the story of Marianne Dashwood's fall. Her tumble takes place when she and her sister Margaret conclude their exploration of the 'high downs' (*SS*: 49) in the countryside around their new home in Devon with an exhilarating downhill run towards their garden gate. The landscape of 'high downs' in this context provides a visual clue to the dynamic of euphoric elevation and demoralizing comedown that Marianne will experience physically when she loses her footing – and psychologically when she falls for the man who is on hand to 'save' her from her fall, John Willoughby. Two forms of accident collide in this scene: the physical mishap of Marianne's tumble and the fortuitous presence of Willoughby to scoop her up, carry her home and ingratiate himself with 'the family to whom accident had now introduced him' (*SS*: 55). Accident at this point in the narrative seems to have come into its own as a storyteller – it is shaping the plot, making the introductions and foreshadowing the moral lessons that the novel has in store for its heroine. Dangerously addicted to the 'highs' of sensibility, Marianne will repeatedly be brought down to earth by the disillusioning events of the novel's plot.

When a woman falls in Austen there is usually a man on hand to catch – or nearly catch – her. Mr Dixon saves Jane Fairfax; Willoughby gathers up Marianne Dashwood; Wentworth lets Louisa Musgrove slip through his fingers. The immediate outcomes of these masculine saviour moments are strikingly different but the overall pattern is the same. The falls in question all take place outdoors and are associated with sociable fun, giddy exhilaration or incautious playfulness. But all three fallers, whether or not they are physically intercepted, will eventually be 'caught' by the wider structures of patriarchy – that is, they will in the aftermath of the accident be re-positioned as creatures of low-**risk** domestic spaces. Louisa Musgrove's short journey from the seaside to the sickbed thus marks an itinerary that many Austen heroines will follow, from active participation in wide-open spaces of pleasure to a chastened existence as a passive creature of confined domesticity.

Life after accidents can be a grey and joyless imitation of what went before. Tom Bertram, the wayward and hedonistic prodigal son of Mansfield Park, leads a dutifully quiet existence in his father's house after recovering from his fall. For the post-accident Louisa Musgrove, there is 'no running or jumping about, no laughing or dancing' (*P*: 237). In the absence of running, jumping, laughing and dancing we can imagine that she has plenty of time to ponder the lessons of her accident and to regret the wayward behaviour that led to its happening in the first place.

In Austen's world, accidents deliver painful lessons about the limits of pleasure. Her fiction imparts an 'accidental' moral education with varying levels of subtlety, but some characters are more than happy to amplify what her narratives of mishap and injury only imply. 'I am very sorry you met with your accident', says *Sanditon*'s Lady Denham to her **friend** and business partner Thomas Parker after his carriage overturns, 'but upon my word you deserved it' (*LM*: 171).

B IS FOR BATH

When Austen learned that her family were planning to move to Bath after her father's retirement, she fainted – or so the family legend goes. The story is possibly apocryphal, and its meanings have been contested (Lee 2007), but there is no doubt that this historic Somerset spa town had a powerful and enduring impact on the author's life, imagination and fiction. The Bath that Austen knew was an artefact of fairly recent architectural and economic history. An extraordinary construction boom in the eighteenth century, one that was in part facilitated by money that flowed from the slave trade, saw the expansion and transformation of a walled medieval town into an elegant, modern health resort and tourist destination, second only to London as a venue for **theatre**, shopping and fashionable sociability. Its most recognizable architectural feature, the Royal Crescent, was completed in the year of Austen's birth, and the town was a landmark in her life and her fiction. Her parents were married there in St Swithin's church in April 1764. Her maternal aunt, **Jane** Leigh-Perrot, used to winter there and stayed loyal to the place even after she was cleared of the charge of shoplifting twenty shillings' worth of white lace from a linen-drapers' on Bath Street. Austen visited Bath in 1797 and 1799, and the family moved there in 1801 following her father's departure from his role as rector of Steventon parish in Hampshire. It was an unsettled and uncertain time for the family. They changed addresses four times in five years, and finally moved on in 1806, a year after George Austen's death. Two years later, Jane was still delightedly recalling her 'happy feelings of Escape!' (*L*: 144) on their departure from Bath.

Bath's unhappy associations of poverty, displacement and bereavement seem to have coincided with a lean spell in Austen's creativity. Her first three major novels, *Northanger Abbey*, *Sense and Sensibility* and *Pride and Prejudice*, were substantially completed during a burst of creativity in the 1790s, while the major works of her mature period, *Mansfield Park*, *Emma* and *Persuasion*, were written from 1811 onwards. The Bath years do not appear to have yielded much aside from a novel-fragment, *The Watsons*, which Austen seems to have abandoned because of its associations with her father's death. Even so, while Austen did not write a great deal in Bath she wrote a great deal about it. Teeming with detailed and discriminating knowledge of its streets, neighbourhoods and architecture, her **letters** from the town are the work of someone who knows far more than you would ever want to know about Bath real estate. These letters bridle energetically at the narrowness and mediocrity of the social scene in Bath: 'Another stupid party last night' (*L*: 89), she writes to Cassandra, after one uninspiring get-together. Her stingingly unimpressed report of another social event – 'There was a monstrous deal of stupid quizzing, & common-place nonsense talked, but scarcely any Wit' (*L*: 108) – has some of the satirical edge that will characterize her fictional representations of the spa town.

Bath's Pump Rooms, streets, houses, shops, theatres, assembly rooms, gardens, concert halls and hotels provide the setting for much of Austen's fiction, from early tales such as 'Jack and Alice', 'The Three Sisters' and 'Love and Freindship' through to the major works that book-end her career as a novelist, *Northanger Abbey* and *Persuasion*. As a rule, when Austen writes about Bath in these texts she writes *against* it. Repeatedly, the town is envisioned in her writings as a scene of intoxicatingly fatuous bustle, a place where newcomers are briefly dazzled by a brilliant mirage of social excitement that soon fades into something oppressively humdrum. Catherine Morland's early experiences of Bath in *Northanger Abbey* provide one representative version of this story of anti-climax: 'Every morning now brought its regular duties; – shops were to be visited; some new part of the town to be looked at; and the Pump-room to be attended, where they paraded up and down for an hour, looking at every body and speaking to no one' (*NA*: 17). There are worse ways to spend your time than shopping and sight-seeing, but when such activities are so routinized and depersonalized then Bath's attractions begin to seem anything but attractive.

With a street-level feel for the town's landmarks and thoroughfares Austen writes on Bath like a dissident tour guide who uses the town's primary attractions to diagnose everything that is wrong with the place. Visitors flock to the theatre, for example, but Austen's Bath-set fictions often suggest that the town as a whole is a kind of large-scale play-house in which two-faced performers such as Isabella Thorpe in *Northanger Abbey* or William Elliot in *Persuasion* carry themselves in charmingly and deceptively manipulative ways. In an environment that seems to foster and even reward superficial and temporary acquaintance, and to prize charm over sincerity and fashion over authenticity, Austen's Bath is over-run by charlatans, role-players and opportunists.

Bath's vaunted status as a destination for shopping and consumer culture also comes in for sceptical scrutiny. Bath was, as Jocelyn Harris notes, the 'first modern city to be designed expressly for shopping' (2007: 184), and Austen herself describes it as a place 'where everything may be purchased' (*L*: 71). The excitable talk of hats, gloves, ribbons and muslins that pervades *Northanger Abbey* testifies to the importance of consumerism in Bath, and this new culture of recreational shopping seems harmless enough – except when it extends into the conduct of romantic relationships. The entire town is a spectacular hub for the Regency marriage market, a place where unattached people go shopping for partners, and where ingenuous **young** women such as Catherine Morland can find themselves 'shopped around' for appraisal by potential husbands. For all the talk of hats and ribbons, the key commodity in *Northanger Abbey* is a heroine whose uncertain market value – is she a fabulously wealthy heiress or a penniless husband-hunter? – is subject to wild fluctuations. The entry of Austen's heroine into Bath society is thus not simply a traditional coming-of-age story but a modern becoming-a-commodity story in which Catherine finds herself in the shop window of a system where 'everything may be purchased'.

Austen also turns a withering diagnostic gaze on Bath's credentials as a centre for health and well-being. In the eighteenth century, rival physicians looking to drum up business engaged in lively controversies over the composition and curative properties of Bath's mineral waters (see Coley 1982), but Austen is decidedly sceptical about any and every claim made for the superior healthfulness of the town's natural and cultural resources. Bath may be a health resort, her fiction implies, but that doesn't mean it's good for you. The place is literally toxic in her early tale 'Jack and Alice', where the seventeen-year-old Lucy is poisoned by a jealous rival. Elsewhere, Bath is in the grip of a cultural toxicity associated with leisure, idleness and narcissistic self-display, a privileging of superficial acquaintance over genuine friendship and short-term novelty over established tradition. Bath is not where people go to get better but rather to indulge their worst selves. If you were to construct a rogues' gallery of the worst people in Austen's fiction then most of its members would have some association with Bath. Willoughby in *Sense and Sensibility*, Wickham in *Pride and Prejudice*, Henry Crawford and Admiral Crawford in *Mansfield Park* and Mr and Mrs Elton in *Emma* are all at some stage reported as having spent time there.

It's a curious detail that, with the exception of the absurd hero of her teenage fragment 'Mr Clifford', no one – likeable or dislikeable – in Austen is ever *from* Bath. The town doesn't seem to function as a point of origin or a dwelling-place but rather as a superficially attractive destination that reveals itself as a swanky open-air prison. Anne Elliot, who went to school in Bath for three years after her mother's death, and who wintered there after her rupture from Wentworth, formulates this most explicitly as she dolefully anticipates an 'imprisonment of many months' (*P*: 148) on her return. Nor are Austen's characters the only ones who feel 'imprisoned' by Bath. Austen's writerly imagination often feels confined and defined by the spa town. Even when she doesn't write about Bath she writes about Bath. The action of *Emma*, for example, goes nowhere near Bath, but Bath wants to come to the novel in the person of the overbearing Mrs Elton, who sweeps into Highbury full of her 'Bath life' and 'Bath habits' (*E*: 297, 313).

It *should* be easy not to write about – or talk about – Bath, but the subject has a curiously insistent way of making itself heard. When Catherine Morland first meets Henry Tilney in the Lower Rooms they enter into easy and pleasant conversation about a variety of subjects before he makes a mock-apology for his failure to ask her the standard Bath questions: 'I have not yet asked you', he archly declares, 'how long you have been in Bath; whether you were ever here before; whether you have been at the Upper Rooms, the theatre, and the concert; and how you like the place altogether' (*NA*: 17–18). No conversation with a Bath newcomer is complete without a ritualized rehearsal of stock questions about the town, and Tilney proceeds to pose these very questions to Austen's bemused heroine.

Henry's awkwardly witty spoofing of the conversational habits of Bath is an attempt to put some ironic distance between himself and a subject that can seem inescapably ubiquitous. Elsewhere, Austen's characters seem eager to put literal distance between themselves and Bath. 'I get so immoderately sick of Bath' (*NA*: 68), says Isabella Thorpe in a letter to Catherine. 'Thank God!', she later exclaims, 'we leave this vile place tomorrow' (*NA*: 222). An air of above-it-all jadedness is de rigueur among veterans of the Bath social scene. It seems important to remind people that Bath isn't everything – that you could, if you wished, be somewhere else. Such protestations have a revealing hollowness. No one in Austen is more imprisoned by Bath – by its styles, habits and ideologies – than those who loudly fantasize about their imminent departure. Only someone with a strong sense of attachment to Bath would make such an elaborate fuss about how disenchanted they are with the place.

Austen's Bath-related writings are strongly attached to the fantasy of 'happy escape' from the place, a moment of transcendence when the spa town will be definitively consigned to the past. When Catherine joins Henry and Eleanor Tilney on a pedestrian excursion to nearby Beechen Cliff, our heroine seems to achieve an enviable vantage-point from which she can catch 'the last view of Bath without any regret' (*NA*: 159). However, such is the persistence of Bath in Austen's imagination that it seems she can never quite take a 'last view' of the place. To the extent that she can't leave behind the fantasy of leaving the place behind, she never quite relinquishes her honorary citizenship of Bath. Her attachment to the place is curiously unshakeable – and demoralizingly so, if we accept the view that she regarded the place as a kind of dystopia (Harris 2007: 187). But Austen's vision of Bath is not quite so determinedly adversarial as some readers have made out. *Persuasion*, for all at that it rehearses familiar notions of Bath as shallow, phony and carceral, nevertheless works towards a more productively ambivalent view of the city. The space of Bath in this novel is not simply an odious fait accompli but a set of social processes and possibilities in which her heroine discovers a life that wasn't available for her in the comparatively static world of the country house. The familiar Bath experiences are still there: a flow of strangers through bustling social spaces; chance encounters and near-misses in the streets, shops, theatres and concert halls; endless claims on one's attention among a roster of competing social possibilities. Such experiences were draining and unsatisfactory in *Northanger Abbey* but in *Persuasion* Austen begins to wonder if there might be different ways of experiencing and moving through Bath. It helps that in this novel the streets of Bath are now thronged by sailors, veterans of the Napoleonic Wars whose easy, relaxed manners and cheerful gregariousness model a different way of inhabiting and moving through the town. Admiral and Mrs Croft, in particular, take to Bath as a place for milling around, bumping into people, and enjoying informal, unscripted social encounters on its unpoliced walkways and street corners. Anne and Wentworth, who have contrived to miss each other in the country and at the seaside, discover in Bath a space in which they can finally rediscover one another. Everything that counted against the place – the crowds, the flow of bodies, the social impermanence – seems to create tantalizing opportunities to bring Austen's protagonists together. Crucially, it is the 'quick-changing, unsettled scene' (*P*: 240) at the Musgroves' rooms in the White Hart inn that provides a context for Wentworth to scribble and surreptitiously deliver the life-changing **letter** that conveys his true feelings to Anne.

Austen's writings often dwell on the demoralizing inescapability of Bath – its prison-like qualities, its deadening ubiquity as a topic of conversation, its culture of narcissistic superficiality – with an **eye** on exit-strategies and escape routes. In *Persuasion* Austen's distaste for Bath is expressed as sharply as ever, but the town is no longer envisaged simply as a place to leave. This is a novel in which the flow and changeability of the town become the conditions of possibility for the renewal of a relationship whose future, we can assume, will by no means be confined to Bath. *Persuasion*'s vision of the spa town is liberating precisely because Austen, at long last, can write about Bath without letting herself be taken prisoner by fantasies of escape.

C IS FOR CHILDREN

Where – and who – are all the children in Austen? If these questions are tricky to answer, it's not because children are absent from her writings. Catherine Morland in *Northanger Abbey* has nine siblings, Fanny Price in *Mansfield Park* is one of eight, while Mr Willmot, the prosperous Sussex landowner in Austen's early tale 'Edgar and Emma', has over twenty sons and daughters. Even when it boasts a sizeable cast of youngsters, however, Austen's fiction does not centre on them in any sustained way. A reader well-versed in Austen might call to mind the children of the Gardiners in *Pride and Prejudice*, or of John and Isabella Knightley in *Emma*, or of John and Anne Musgrove in *Persuasion* but they might struggle to retrieve specifics about the supporting cast of pre-teen cousins, nephews and nieces who caper around the edges of these adult-centred texts.

Children seem, on the face of it, to be second-class citizens in Austen's narrative worlds. They are plentiful enough but they are not always carefully individuated; they can be noisy but they are not given much in the way of intelligible dialogue; they can be hyperactive but their doings are not shaped into storylines whose outcomes we are invested in; they intrude on our notice not as autonomous beings but as reflections of their parents' shortcomings (Selwyn 2010: 110). For some readers (Auerbach 1986; Ricks 1996), the apparent marginality of infants in Austen's writings raises the question of whether she 'liked' children. It's a loaded and not particularly helpful question – you might as well ask if she 'liked' people (some days more than others, probably). It does however seem fair to observe that Austen's fiction wants us to dislike people who don't like children. Early reports in *Mansfield Park* that Mrs Norris 'never knew how to be pleasant to children' (*MP*: 29) prove to be an appallingly accurate understatement about Fanny Price's aunt. Feigned affection for children – such as is exhibited by the Steele sisters towards Lady Middleton's children in *Sense and Sensibility* – is easy enough to see through. Genuine fondness for children, of the kind shown by, say, **Jane** Bennett in *Pride and Prejudice* or Admiral Croft in *Persuasion*, is normally a good sign of humour and humanity.

But fond and accommodating attentiveness to children, however warmly Austen seems to approve of it, does not seem to be built into the architecture of her storylines. Most of her novels belong to the coming-of-age or coming out genre – that is, they are texts where people become story-worthy precisely at the moment when they are no longer defined as children. This is one reason why disused childhood spaces such as the old school-room occupied by Fanny Price in *Mansfield Park* or the deserted nursery at Uppercross in *Persuasion* have a resonantly understated significance in the world of her novels. Narrative begins in Austen when childhood ends. And even if the desire was there to centre on a school-age demographic, there is something curiously narrative-resistant about children. The life of a child – 'all the eating and drinking, and sleeping and playing' (*E*: 99) – is too creaturely, too in-the-moment and one-dimensional, to merit the kind of searching, nuanced representations of choice, decision, anticipation and retrospection that comprise narratable adult experience for Austen.

If children seem to be a non-subject for Austen the novelist, they can still provoke endless talk among her less gifted conversationalists. 'On every formal **visit** a child ought to be of the party', the narrator drily remarks in *Sense and Sensibility*, 'by way of provision for discourse' (*SS*: 37). Such discourse is of dependably poor quality. Nowhere in Austen is child-related dialogue more spectacularly banal than in the spirited dispute that breaks out at the Dashwoods' London residence about whether Harry Dashwood is taller than William Middleton. Sadly we'll never know who was right. Austen's sympathies are evidently with Marianne Dashwood, who is unable even to fake an opinion on this inane controversy. Austen isn't interested in the outcome of the dispute, but she is interested in what the dispute reveals about adult attitudes to children. In this scene, adults who profess to care about the individuality of children can express themselves only with recourse to a quantitative language in which children are experienced as rival sets of numbers.

Sometimes it is sheer force of numbers that seems to disqualify children from narrative representation, as when Catherine Morland's siblings are glimpsed as a scrum of 'heads and arms and legs' (*NA*: 5) or when the sons and daughters of Mr Willmot in 'Edgar and Emma' are deemed to be 'too numerous to be particularly described' (*J*: 34). The very qualities that give them a claim on our attention can become the grounds on which they are ignored or sidelined. 'Here are Children in abundance' (*LM*: 10), writes the titular heroine of *Lady Susan*, when she arrives at the home of her in-laws, the Vernons. She promises to learn the names of her hosts' children, but there is no evidence that she ever gets round to doing so; nor, it has to be said, do we ever learn how many children the Vernons have or what their names are. *Lady Susan* both satirizes and replicates its heroine's seeming indifference to the text's non-adult characters.

Every so often, however, children in Austen attract attention as people rather than as numbers. In *The Watsons* we see a child on the dancefloor, of all places. When little Charles Blake – a ten-year-old boy who loves dancing – is left unpartnered at a ball, our heroine Emma Watson steps in and kindly offers to **dance** with him. This episode grants a **young** boy what is, by Austen's standards, an unusually generous amount of narrative space. Concluding with Charles's eager request that Emma visit Osborne Castle, there to behold a 'monstrous curious stuffed fox [...] and a badger' (*LM*: 100), it is a memorable and scene-stealing moment for Emma's young **friend**, quite unlike any other child-centred episode in Austen. But this intriguing detour through child-centred experience rapidly finds its way back to an adult-centred storyline. Emma's dance with little Charles functions primarily as a mechanism that brings her into a new range of adult relationships – it wins her the grateful friendship of Charles's mother and the admiring attention of a number of unattached men at the dance, including Mr Howard, Tom Musgrave and Lord Osborne. What is more, Charles seems to be a kind of diminutive proxy for Emma's grown-up admirers. When he exclaims, 'Oh! Uncle, do look at my partner. She is so pretty!' (*LM*: 99), he unselfconsciously proclaims what is already being covertly whispered about Emma's looks and desirability among her new audience at the assembly rooms. Charles is not simply a charmingly incongruous dance partner, then, but an intermediary who brokers Emma's entry into a new social circle – and an innocent mouthpiece for the desires that she will provoke in that circle.

Charles Blake comes into his own – albeit briefly – as a substantive character when he conducts himself like a miniature adult, an impeccably behaved little gentleman on the dancefloor. Elsewhere in Austen, boisterous disruptiveness in children is more likely than exemplary conduct to claim narrative attention. Infants in her writings are responsible for small outbreaks of anarchy in her elegant social spaces. There are plenty of military men in Austen, but the most conspicuously violent people in her fiction are the children. Typical in this regard are Fanny Price's 'untameable' (*MP*: 452) siblings whose uncontrollably rowdy behaviour provides such a jolting contrast to the serene domestic world of Mansfield Park. The sight of her siblings 'kicking each other's shins [...] immediately under their father's **eye**' (*MP*: 443) is one indication that children's violent conduct in

Austen is usually a symptom of lax or negligent parenting. Austen attends to children precisely when their parents' vigilance is at its most forgivingly unfocused. Lady Middleton in *Sense and Sensibility* deserves special mention in this regard, calmly looking on as her children play havoc with her cousins' personal effects: 'She saw their [the Miss Steeles'] sashes untied, their hair pulled about their ears, their work-bags searched, and their knives and scissars [*sic*] stolen away' (*SS*: 139). As we marvel at their capacity for destruction, it is worth asking – where exactly are the children in this sentence? Vanishing behind a string of passive verbs ('untied … pulled … searched … stolen'), the agency of the little Middletons is envisioned primarily in terms of its gremlin-like effects on adult bodies and property.

Among children's general talent for mayhem in Austen there is a particular and slightly worrying interest in bladed instruments. Just as the little Middletons make off with the Miss Steeles' knives and scissors, so Fanny Price's sisters will squabble over a silver knife (*MP*: 446) and Mr Woodhouse will be alarmed when his grandson, little Henry Knightley, asks for a knife (*E*: 86). The figure of the weaponized or potentially weaponized child gives a certain vivid trenchancy to Austen's perception that children already have an even stronger weapon at their disposal: the auditory violence of noise. From the 'violent screams' of Annmaria Middleton in *Sense and Sensibility* (*SS*: 140) to the 'thumping and hallooing' (*SS*: 442) that reverberate through the Price household in *Mansfield Park* to the 'clamour of the children' (*P*: 146) that drowns out adult conversation in *Persuasion*, the uproar of infants is an ear-splitting ordeal for Austen's more refined and fastidious heroines. Noise of this sort is also the enemy of language as Austen deploys it. In the world of her fiction, where so much depends on ironic reserve, subtle understatement and resonant silence, those infantile screams and halloos represent a kind of linguistic anti-matter in which everything that makes Austen's literary voice audible is drowned out.

With those screams ringing in its ears, Austen's fiction toys ambivalently with various fantasies of a 'child-free world' (Auerbach 1986: 177). Sometimes this world is experienced as a dream of escape, as when Lady Russell gratefully exchanges the child-generated din of Uppercross for the enlivening hubbub of **Bath**. Elsewhere, a horror of routine proximity to children is registered with a sympathetic shudder. When Elizabeth Watson declares that she 'would rather do any thing than be a teacher at a school' (*LM*: 83), she speaks for many Austen characters – the respectable, educated women whose uncertain financial prospects mean that they may be obliged to work with children for a living. The exemplary member of this precarious group is **Jane** Fairfax in *Emma*. No less accomplished than the novel's privileged heroine, Jane is seemingly destined for a career as a governess – hardly a fate worse than death, but a demoralizing prospect in the world of a novelist who lays such emphasis on the raucous ungovernability of children.

A more subtle version of Jane Fairfax's dismaying trajectory towards a career in childcare is represented by Austen's exploration of the aunt-role as it is inhabited by characters such as Emma Woodhouse and Anne Elliot. The heroines of *Emma* and *Persuasion* are set apart from the other major Austen heroines in the respect that they are already aunts when these novels get underway. Little nephews and nieces are already a vibrant and fun part of their lives, and it seems entirely possible that the life of an aunt – playing with and ministering to the children of their sisters – is what they will settle for instead of a romantic life. Anne in particular is frequently defined in terms of her usefulness as nurse and child-minder, and seems early in the novel to be tethered to childcare responsibilities that will inhibit her own flourishing as a free-standing character. It is significant, therefore, that at key moments in *Emma* and *Persuasion* the heroine is smoothly, unexpectedly – and gratifyingly – disburdened of a young child. When Emma is dandling her eight-month-old niece, Mr Knightley takes the baby out of her arms 'with all the unceremoniousness of perfect amity' (*E*: 105). In *Persuasion*, when little Walter Musgrove clambers all over Anne Elliot, he is smoothly borne away by Wentworth, leaving Austen's heroine 'speechless […] with most disordered feelings' (*P*: 87). At this point, a euphorically flustered Anne has been divested of her role as de facto governess or unpaid childcare assistant – and given the chance to decide who she is and what she wants to be. She has been freed from the burden of a child – but this does not mean that she has become a citizen of a world without children. In both of these scenes the person who unburdens the heroine is the man whom she will eventually marry – that is, if we follow the official teleology of Austen's narratives, the man who will likely become the father of her children. It is precisely because the world of Austen's fiction is never quite child-free that it is so receptive to these brief, intense fantasies of freedom from children.

D IS FOR DANCE

'People that dance', says Catherine Morland in *Northanger Abbey*, 'only stand opposite each another in a long room for half an hour' (*NA*: 74). It is a mildly startling thing for an Austen heroine to say, so comprehensively does it underestimate all the ways in which dance matters in Austen – as a source of pleasure in physical movement, as a practice of communal self-display, as an opportunity for the exchange of private words in a public space, as a socially permissible form of physical proximity between men and women, and as a respectable context for courtship and flirtation. If you are ever in any doubt about who the significant love interests are for the heroine of an Austen novel, you need only look at her dance partners. Catherine is dancing with the man whom she will eventually marry within four sentences of meeting him.

Little as *Northanger Abbey*'s heroine seems to recognize it, then, dance in Austen can be a form of 'sexualized social interaction' (Malone 2016: 428) that is also a 'business deal' (Sulloway 1989: 138). The dancefloor is where men and women meet each other, but also where her great themes of love and money encounter each other, ostensibly in search of nothing more than the sheer pleasure of choreographed movement to music. Beyond all of this, dance has a figurative existence in her work, as when the heroine of *Emma* finds herself in 'dancing, singing, exclaiming spirits' (*E*: 518) as her story moves to a happy conclusion or when Anne Elliot and Captain Wentworth declare their enduring love for one another with 'spirits dancing in private rapture' (*P*: 261). But maybe Catherine Morland has a point. If people were conscious of its enormous significance, they probably wouldn't be very good at dancing – and they certainly wouldn't enjoy it.

A dance in Austen can take the form of an impromptu set at home, as with the Lucases in *Pride and Prejudice* or the Coles in *Emma*. Or it could be a formal ball hosted by an eminent local citizen, such as those hosted by Bingley at Netherfield or Sir Thomas Bertram at Mansfield Park. Or it could be a larger event in a public space such as the assembly rooms in **Bath** (*Northanger Abbey*) or the Crown Inn in Highbury (*Emma*). Film and television adaptations of Austen have given us – accurately or otherwise – a lavish visual sense of how dance was conducted in Austen's world, but her books are curiously un-vivid in their depiction of dancers in action. Someone who came to Austen's work knowing nothing at all about social dance in the Georgian era would glean only the haziest sense of what the activity looks like in practice. What exactly is a cotillion ball (*NA*: 70)? What is the formation for a Boulanger (*PP*: 13)? Austen's fiction doesn't tell us – or, rather, it assumes that its early nineteenth-century audience doesn't need to be told. No one will ever learn to dance from a Jane Austen novel.

A rare physical evocation of dance in Austen focuses on a character's missteps. In *Pride and Prejudice*, Elizabeth's ordeal of dancing with Mr Collins is compounded by her partner's habit of 'moving wrong without being aware of it' (*PP*: 101). Rehearsed in Collins's clumsy dance moves is his blundering progress through a novel in which he will make one blissfully unselfaware *faux pas* after another. Another close-up of a dancer in action turns out to be a false memory. In *Mansfield Park*, when William Price remarks that he hasn't had the pleasure of seeing his sister dance since she was a little girl, Henry Crawford is prepared to report having seen Fanny 'gliding about with quiet, light elegance, and in admirable time' (*MP*: 291). That certainly seems like a fair description of how Fanny Price would dance, doesn't it? Except that, as Crawford admits to himself, he has no such memory because he wasn't paying attention the first time Fanny danced in his presence. But neither, it has to be said, was Austen herself.

Austen's fiction attaches tremendous significance to dance even as it keeps a certain guarded distance from the physicality of dance and from the bodies of dancers. Darcy is at his most off-puttingly supercilious when he scornfully remarks that 'Every savage can dance' (*PP*: 28) but Austen's fiction doesn't absolutely repudiate the thinking behind his remark. The links between dance, physicality and untamed desire are obvious enough, even in the refined world of the Austen ballroom, to stir and trouble her imagination. One function of a ball in her social worlds is as a mechanism for the social management of potentially unruly desires. Social dancing caters for – but also aims to regulate and contain – the powerful appetites for exhilarating physical excitement exhibited by those who, like the Musgrove sisters in *Persuasion*, are 'wild for dancing' (*P*: 51). In the Austen ballroom, the 'savagery' or wildness of erotic desire is contained within strictly choreographed patterns of movement and showcased as being at the heart of the most elegantly civilized public behaviour.

Nowhere in Austen are relations of status, hierarchy and precedence more formally paraded and stringently enforced than on the dancefloor. Powerful unwritten rules govern who can and can't be invited, who can address whom, who leads the dances and who dances with whom. In *Northanger Abbey*, the rules of the dancefloor dictate that Catherine has to decline an invitation to dance with a man she very much likes (Henry Tilney) because she has already agreed to dance with a man she dislikes (John Thorpe). In *Emma* there is no question that Mrs Elton, hardly the toast of Highbury, 'must be asked to begin the ball' (*E*: 351) at the Crown Inn because she is a recent bride. When hierarchical relations of power, submission and control are dressed up in fine clothes and set to music, then you can begin to see why one critic has cautioned readers against getting too swept away by the 'fascination of ballroom fascism' (O'Farrell 1997: 154 n. 21) in Austen.

If dance is nothing more than a ritual performance of existing social hierarchies, however, then we need to ask why two of the most powerful men in Austen's fiction seem conspicuously reluctant to step onto the dancefloor. Darcy in *Pride and Prejudice* and Knightley in *Emma* are the richest and most distinguished men in their respective novels, but both are notably unenthusiastic about dance. When the dancing gets underway, these two powerful but stand-offish landowners hover on the sidelines with self-conscious dignity. For Darcy and Knightley, dance seems to entail a degree of reputational and/or emotional **risk**. It wouldn't do to be seen to be dancing with the 'wrong' person, especially if that dance partner is beguilingly attractive. Dance, for men of property and substance, also has potentially demeaning associations with the **young** – that is, with flighty, unsettled and unproven characters such as Frank Churchill. Even though social dancing is a celebration of the status quo, powerful men such as Darcy and Knightley seem to have more to lose than to gain on the dancefloor.

Austen's reluctant male dancers may hover in splendid isolation on the edge of the dancefloor, but they are given significant symbolic 'partners' or countertypes in the broader structures of the novels. Darcy is usually accompanied by his **friend** Bingley, a people-pleasing sidekick who loves to dance. Knightley, meanwhile, is carefully counterpointed with his bête noire, Frank Churchill, a veritable impresario for dance, music and vivacious sociability in Highbury. Whereas Darcy and Knightley are reluctant to sacrifice personal gravitas to collective pleasure, Austen's enthusiastic male dancers have no such inhibitions. 'Nothing but Dancing here – ' (*J*: 273) is the hopeful enquiry of the glamorous newcomer Edward Stanley in 'Catharine, or the Bower' as he breezes into the neighbourhood, a kind of anti-Darcy who wants to establish his social identity on the dancefloor rather than in the drawing-room. Whereas men of means, substance and authority in Austen may not feel the need to dance, there are those who, whether because they are outsiders (like Frank Churchill), or second sons (like Henry Tilney), or **poor** (like Willoughby in *Sense and Sensibility*), have 'Nothing but dancing' to make their mark.

It may seem, then, that there are two types of men in Austen: the under- and the over-enthusiastic dancers. But this simple division points to a deeper ambivalence within those key male characters such as Darcy and Knightley who ultimately seem to combine both traits. In this context, the question of what it will take to get Darcy and Knightley dancing is never less than intriguing. In both *Pride and Prejudice* and *Emma*, the pre-dance manoeuvrings – what has been called the 'dance-before-the-dance' (Dow Adams 1982: 61) – are elaborate. Darcy and Elizabeth orbit one another, or dance round one another, cagey but intrigued in the early chapters of *Pride and Prejudice*, while the first half of *Emma* can be read as a build up to the moment when the heroine asks Mr Knightley to ask her to dance (*E*: 358). It is notable that, for all Darcy's seeming stand-offishness, when Elizabeth does finally dance with him it is on the third time of asking. When Emma dances with Knightley, meanwhile, it is in the aftermath of his decision to dance with Harriet Smith. Knightley's dance with Harriet is often interpreted as a gesture of sheer altruistic **kindness**, but who's to say he didn't very much enjoy dancing with an attractive young woman, not least as a means of appearing to best advantage in the **eyes** of Emma?

The primary narratable substance of any dance, in Austen, is the dialogue that it makes possible. In a social world where opportunities for one-to-one conversation at close quarters between members of the opposite sex are extraordinarily rare, every word in these situations counts. John Thorpe spectacularly bungles his opportunity to impress Catherine as he rattles on about '**horses** and dogs' (*NA*: 50) during their dance. The in-dance conversation between Elizabeth and Darcy is altogether more complex and uneasy:

> They stood for some time without speaking a word; and she began to imagine that their silence was to last through the two dances, and at first was resolved not to break it; till suddenly fancying that it would be the greater punishment to her partner to oblige him to talk, she made some slight observation on the dance. He replied, and was silent again. After a pause of some minutes, she addressed him a second

time with'It is *your* turn to say something now, Mr Darcy. – *I* talked about the dance, and *you* ought to make some kind of remark on the size of the room, or the number of couples.'

(PP: 102)

Mansell points out that there can be no suspense about the outcome of a dance (1973: 8–9) but the same is not true in this interlude of dialogue between Elizabeth and Darcy, in which a tense stand-off will evolve into a flirtatious *tête-à-tête* that becomes an escalating war of words. It is an exchange in which, crucially, neither party controls the tone or the outcome, and whose effects will continue to work themselves out long after this particular set has concluded. Dance has brought them closer without eliminating the many **obstacles** between them.

Austen's grand characters often step nervously onto the dancefloor – and perhaps the grandest of all, Lord Osborne in *The Watsons*, is simply unwilling to dance (he uses Tom Musgrave as a proxy or body double on the dancefloor). But we shouldn't overstate the democratic or subversive possibilities of dance in her fiction. Her ballroom scenes certainly don't amount to anything like a carnivalesque free-for-all. Decorum is nearly always maintained. We don't see **servants**, tradesmen or the poor on dancefloor, and the participation of a child in the ball in *The Watsons* is a delightful one-off. Even so, within those limitations, the movement of dance can open up subtle possibilities for other kinds of movement, as when Frank Churchill uses the ball to create his own alternative to the Knightley–Woodhouse axis in Highbury, or when Darcy finds in Elizabeth Bennet a dance partner who isn't overawed by his rank and reputation. A dance is, by definition, a circular movement, one that ends where it begins, but Austen is always alert to the possibility of new directions in a journey that goes nowhere.

E IS FOR EYE

'[H]er eyes were here, there, every where' (*NA*: 11). The eyes in question belong to Catherine Morland, newly arrived from a Wiltshire village and eagerly taking in the variety and spectacle of **Bath**. To a remarkable extent, *Northanger Abbey* is the story of Catherine's eyes – what they see, what they don't see, what she thinks they see and how her insights are conditioned by the Gothic fiction that she so avidly devours. Austen's heroine is a voracious, wide-eyed and naive onlooker in a novel that will keenly monitor the symbolic insights achieved in and through her humiliating misperceptions.

Nor is *Northanger Abbey* the only Austen novel with a focus on optical experience. Eyes, once we start looking for them, are 'here, there, every where' in her work. In *Sense and Sensibility*, Elinor Dashwood is acutely conscious of the 'little sharp eyes' (*SS*: 167), the predatory watchfulness, of her problematic **friend** and romantic rival Lucy Steele. Much of *Pride and Prejudice* revolves around what Elizabeth and Darcy see – or think they see – in one another's eyes. *Emma*, a book-length comedy about not seeing what's there in plain sight, makes a sly joke about its own optical obsessions when it lets us glimpse its most artfully misdirective character hard at work mending a pair of spectacles (*E*: 259). More broadly, Austen's novels, especially in their key scenes of **dance** and communal sociability, are about the coming-into-visibility of their **young** female protagonists. Her heroines peer eagerly into a wider social landscape – and the world, in turn, captures them in its appraising gaze. Typical in this regard is the celebrity enjoyed in *The Watsons* by Emma the morning after the ball at D-: '[E]verybody wanted to look again at the girl who had been admired the night before by Lord Osborne –. Many were the eyes, and various the degrees of approbation with which she was examined' (*LM*: 106).

Like many Austen heroines, Emma Watson has to come to terms with her own enhanced visibility as the price of entry into an extended social space full of visual thrills and stimulations. For every **Jane** Fairfax, demurely conscious of 'seeing herself watched' (*E*: 378), there be will those like the Miss Beauforts in *Sanditon* whose eye-catching antics are designed to make 'many a gazer gaze again' (*LM*: 203). The 'gazers' in *Sanditon* – and elsewhere in Austen – are implicitly assumed to be men. To be 'out', in her world, is to navigate a world whose social spaces are swept and surveyed by a dominant male gaze. If we are looking for an archetypal male spectator in Austen then we could do worse than alight on a figure who appears just once in her writings. 'Sweet Mr Ogle', she once wrote to Cassandra. 'I dare say he sees all the Panoramas for nothing, has free admittance everywhere; he is so delightful!' (*L*: 259). Who exactly was this wonderfully named person? It turns out that Edward Ogle (*c*.1759–1819) was a Worthing-born entrepreneur with business interests in the **West Indies** who owned a set of barges on the Thames – and was possibly a source for Mr Parker in *Sanditon* (Edmonds 2013). Ogle's barges gave him 'free admittance' to the impressive views of London from the Thames, and his name might almost have been coined to denote a propensity for unabashed looking, a capacity to take in a shameless eyeful of the world around him.

Edward Ogle is never again mentioned in Austen's **letters**, but there are plenty of other intent, powerful male observers to occupy the 'Mr Ogle' role in her fiction, not least in public spaces where there are women to behold. Urban space is a particular haunt for intrusive male spectators in her work. Sometime the male gaze operates at a surreptitious distance from its object. It is difficult to describe Willoughby's furtive surveillance of Marianne Dashwood in London as anything other than stalker-like (*SS*: 370). Elsewhere, male voyeurism is shamelessly undisguised. On a hypercritical quest for a single 'tolerable face' (*P*: 153) in the Bath crowds, Sir Walter Elliot appraises and objectifies women like a roving quality-control inspector. This kind of systematic scrutiny, appraisal and ranking of women in public space – an exemplary case of what Austen's celebrated predecessor Frances Burney refers to as 'face-hunting' – shows us a privileged male gaze at its most predatory and fetishistic.

Of all the male onlookers in Austen, none is more formidable – or seemingly inscrutable – than Darcy in *Pride and Prejudice*. One of the first things that Elizabeth and Darcy notice about each other is their eyes. Darcy is taken by the 'beautiful expression of her dark eyes' (*PP*: 26) while Elizabeth declares that he has a 'very satirical eye' (*PP*: 26). Darcy's interest in Elizabeth, at this point, is superficially appreciative, while Elizabeth's reaction to Darcy – her conjecture about the satirical intent behind his gaze – displays curiosity about his personality and values. Whether Elizabeth is right to say Darcy has a satirical eye is not immediately clear. Given Darcy's air of high-minded seriousness and carefully managed personal dignity, it seems surprising to associate him with raillery or derisive humour. It seems possible, given her obvious relish for laughter and her pleasure in absurdity, that Elizabeth is seeing herself in Darcy at this point. At the same time, she may well also be glimpsing a redemptive truth about Darcy, a glint of the humour and humanity of a man who, thus far in the novel, has been a prisoner of his own defensive gravitas.

All of this visual excitement and uncertainty in the optical exchanges between Elizabeth and Darcy is to be expected in a text whose working title was *First Impressions*. The difference between at-a-glance knowledge and the kind of insights furnished by deeper and more sustained acquaintance will be explored, continually, through the story of the principals' eyes. As Elizabeth tries to fathom why Darcy's eyes are 'fixed on her' (*PP*: 56), Darcy's candid admiration for her 'fine eyes' (*PP*: 39, 50) will become a standing joke among his acquaintances. When Miss Bingley goadingly asks whether any painter could 'do justice' to Elizabeth's 'beautiful eyes?' Darcy responds unflappably: 'It would not be easy, indeed, to catch their expression, but their colour and shape, and the eye-lashes, so remarkably fine, might be copied' (*PP*: 57). His regard for Elizabeth is undisguised, though it is expressed as connoisseurial appreciation of her appearance rather than emotional attachment to her person. Elizabeth's eyes are what he feels comfortable talking about. What he thinks about her voice – her ready wit and fearless backchat – he keeps to himself. In due course Darcy will steel himself 'not to fix his eyes on Elizabeth' (*PP*: 81), though even this effortful not-looking-at-Elizabeth pays an awkward tribute of deflected attention to the novel's heroine.

There is a curious symmetry in *Pride and Prejudice* between Darcy's strenuously unruffled account of a hypothetical portrait of Elizabeth, and Elizabeth's reaction to an actual portrait of Darcy at Pemberley: '[A]s she stood before the canvas, on which he was represented, and fixed his eyes upon herself, she thought of his regard with a deeper sentiment of gratitude than it had ever raised before; she remembered its warmth, and softened its impropriety of expression' (*PP*: 277). It is often the case in this novel that Darcy is at his best when we can't see him – when he is performing behind-the-scene acts of generosity, solving problems and doing his best to repair the damage wreaked by Wickham. What makes the portrait episode so distinctive is that it finally lets us – and Elizabeth – take a good look at Darcy when he's not there. Except, in an odd moment of perceptual turnaround, the effect here is not of Elizabeth looking at the painting but of the painting looking at her. The male gaze here emanates not from a human eye but from a portrait and everything it represents – the sum total of Darcy's magnificent land, property and possessions at Pemberley. Elizabeth seems to come into a sympathetic rapport with Darcy not when they are eyeball to eyeball but when his gaze is routed back to her through the impersonal intermediary of art.

The gaze in Austen is often at its most powerful when it is routed through a third party. In *Persuasion*, Anne Elliot is appreciatively noticed on the sea-front by a gentleman who will later be identified as her cousin, the charming but odious William Elliot. What makes their exchange of glances so intriguing is the way it draws in a third pair of eyes, those of Captain Wentworth:

> Anne's face caught his eye, and he looked at her with a degree of earnest admiration, which she could not be insensible of. She was looking remarkably well; her very regular, very pretty features, having the bloom and freshness of youth restored by the fine wind which had been blowing on her complexion, and by the animation of eye which it had also produced. It was evident that the gentleman, [...] admired her exceedingly. Captain Wentworth looked round at her instantly in a way which shewed his noticing of it. He gave her a momentary glance, – a glance of brightness, which seemed to say, 'That man is struck with you, – and even I, at this moment, see something like Anne Elliot again.'
>
> (*P*: 112)

It would be difficult to find in Austen's works a neater exemplification of the notion that desire is always imitative (see: Girard 1966). Anne becomes desirable in Wentworth's eyes when he sees her being desired. His visual desire, in other words, is copied and modelled on that of William Elliot. Subsequent revelations in *Persuasion* will confirm William Elliot as one of Austen's most obnoxious villains, but none of that seems to undermine the power of his gaze to bring Anne into a new and revitalizing visibility. It is William Elliot's gaze, as much as the 'fine wind' on the sea-front, that enables Wentworth, in a revelatory moment of déjà vu, to recognize the new/old Anne who was in front of him all along.

But it would be misleading to imply that the Austen heroine is never anything more than an inert object of competing male gazes. Even Austen's most wide-eyed, ingenuous heroine, Catherine Morland, perceives the world in complex and valuable ways. *Northanger Abbey*'s comedy of visual perception often hinges on a discrepancy between Catherine's 'unpractised eye' (*NA*: 170) and Henry Tilney's 'quick eye' (*NA*: 202). Henry has seen more of the world than Catherine. He is alive to deceptive and unscrupulous behaviour in ways that she isn't. His education, moreover, has enabled him to see landscape, architecture, history and books through the enlightening prism of high culture. As it mediates between Catherine and Henry, *Northanger Abbey* achieves a kind of double vision in which the world is simultaneously perceived through the eyes of both naivety and sophistication; it is, to adapt a famous phrase of William Blake's, a novel of optical innocence and experience. However, if *Northanger Abbey* were nothing more than the story of innocence being chasteningly and repeatedly lessoned by experience then it would not be much of a novel. What makes Austen's narrative compelling is its willingness to take Catherine's gaze seriously in all its hectic and ardent extravagance. Everything that she thinks she 'sees' at Northanger Abbey – an oppressive Gothic villain, a sinister family history, traces of misogynistic violence – discloses a truth about General Tilney, and about patriarchy, that the events of the novel corroborate. The truth of Northanger Abbey – and indeed of *Northanger Abbey* – becomes visible only via the Gothicized gaze of Catherine Morland. There is a lot that a complacently sophisticated world can learn from an unpractised eye.

F IS FOR FRIEND

'You are a very strange creature by way of a friend!' (*PP*: 27) says Elizabeth
Bennet to Charlotte Lucas during a party at the latter's family home.
Only a friend could address another friend in this way. Elizabeth's tone
of teasing, quizzical distance from Charlotte is framed and softened by a
context of affectionate and long-standing familiarity between the two; her
arch allegation of strangeness is the very proof of the friends' intimacy. Yet
this small moment of friendly teasing is, nevertheless, revelatory of the
potential for estrangement that so often lurks within amiable relations in
Austen's world. Elizabeth and Charlotte are by no means the only friends
who will become strangers to one another in her novels. More than this,
Elizabeth's gentle taunt is suggestive of the ways in which the very notion
of friendship becomes conceptually strange in Austen. Though it seems to
name a likeably uncomplicated form of human relationship, 'friend', in her
writings, will repeatedly become an oddly problematic term, one that resists
easy definition or evaluation.

'Friend' is a term that was undergoing a notable semantic shift in the
Georgian period. There was a time when it had denoted the circle of
powerful and influential people in one's life, not least senior members of
one's immediate and extended family. A more modern sense of friend as an
intimate companion chosen on the basis of shared pleasures and personal
affinities was gaining ground in the eighteenth century. Much of Samuel
Richardson's great epistolary novel *Clarissa* (1748) hinges on the distinction
between the heroine's 'friends' in the old sense (her appalling extended
family) and her 'friend' in the new sense (the steadfast Anna Howe). Such a
distinction persists well into Austen's fiction, where the figure of the friend
features sometimes in a supervisory or quasi-parental role (think Lady
Russell in *Persuasion*) and sometimes as an intimate companion (think
Eleanor Tilney in *Northanger Abbey*). Austen's fiction can even be read as the
story of the transition between these two models of friendships. *Sense and
Sensibility*, for example, has been described as a novel that enacts the victory
of 'friend-as-intimate over friend-as-benefactor' (Deresiewicz 2004: 99).

Given the semantic complexity of the term, it seems revealingly appropriate that Austen didn't know how to spell 'friendship'. The most substantial of her teenage fictions is a short epistolary novel entitled 'Love and Freindship' and most modern editors keep the misspelling. Despite Austen's orthographic mix-up, 'love and friendship' is a collocation that trips off the tongue, and indeed a title that we could swap with that of any of Austen's major works. From *Northanger Abbey* to *Persuasion*, Austen tells the same story over and over again – a **young** unmarried woman experiences a sudden broadening of her horizons, does a lot of socializing, makes new friends, falls in love and gets married. Along the way, she will have to make two kinds of friendship-related choice. First, she has to learn to discriminate between bad friends and good friends. Just as Austen repeatedly presents her heroines with an either/or choice between two seemingly eligible men – Darcy or Wickham? Knightley or Churchill? Wentworth or William Elliot? – so she likes to confront them with a choice between two potentially compelling candidates for intimate friendship. In *Northanger Abbey*, Catherine Morland ponders the comparative appeal of Isabella Thorpe and Eleanor Tilney, while the heroine of *Emma* wavers between Harriet Smith and **Jane** Fairfax. Of course you might well object that the analogy between romantic choices and friendship choices is a faulty one. In a culture of monogamy, you can officially commit to only one life partner, but who ever said you could only have one friend? On the face of it, the either/or choice between friend A and friend B is a false one that borrows the love-triangle structure in order to lend spurious pointedness to a decidedly non-urgent choice. For Austen, however, the choice isn't simply between one or other friend (between Isabella or Eleanor, say) but between one or other *kind* of friendship. This becomes clearer in *Persuasion* where Anne Elliot's delight in the easy-going sociability of the Crofts and their naval acquaintances represents a firm repudiation of the facsimile of friendship on offer in the snooty, exclusive circles in which her father and sister move.

The second friendship-related choice confronted by the Austen heroine is not between one or other friend, or even one or other mode of friendship, but between friendship itself and romantic love. Many readers (Brownstein 1982; Perry 1986; Thomason 2015) have remarked on the difficulties that beset female friendship in Austen. In a society where unattached women are obliged to compete for eligible men, friends can easily become rivals. Emma Woodhouse's friendships with both Harriet Smith and Jane Fairfax are significantly complicated by the perception that they may harbour a romantic interest in Knightley. At other times, the very possibility of friendship – such as the one that Elizabeth Bennet *might* have struck up with Caroline Bingley – can be precluded by romantic rivalry. The journey towards matrimony in Austen is often traced as a journey away from strained and fracturing female friendships towards a point at which, as Rachel Brownstein puts it, women must 'leave the company of their sex' (1982: 109). Towards the end of an Austen novel, female friends – good and bad alike – tend to melt away as the heroine's life is redefined by and gathered into matrimonial structures that centre on the figure of the husband. From Charlotte Lucas to Mary Crawford to Harriet Smith, Austen's fiction is full of friends whose significance in the heroine's life fades irreversibly once she is on a clear trajectory towards marriage. Even when immersed in the delights of intimate camaraderie, Austen's fiction is haunted always by the *end* in friendship.

Friendships end in different ways. Some fizzle out (Harriet is steadily re-located to the edge of Emma's social circle), some fall victim to circumstance (Fanny Price and Mary Crawford's lives go in different directions) and some are unilaterally cancelled (Catherine Morland stops answering Isabella Thorpe's **letters**). But often it is not simply a case of weeding out one problematic individual from an otherwise flourishing social circle; rather, it is a case of breaking up the entire circle. Austen's fiction charts the rise and fall not simply of friendships but of friendship groups – cliques and in-crowds whose members revel in one another's company for an intense but short-lived period of diverting sociability. Whether we are talking about the mix of friends, family, neighbours and newcomers who convene at Netherfield in *Pride and Prejudice* or the **theatre**-loving youths who take over Mansfield Park in Sir Thomas Bertram's absence, the friendship group becomes a powerful, dynamic social entity in Austen, crackling with repartee, rivalry, open flirtation, unacknowledged desire and frantic social energy. Sometimes those energies transform the family home into a hub of extra-familial sociability, as witness Sir John Middleton's habit of 'for ever forming parties' (*SS*: 39) at Barton Park in *Sense and Sensibility*. But the friendship group often strikes out beyond the family home in search of novelty and stimulation. Schemes and excursions – to Bristol in *Northanger Abbey*, to Sotherton in *Mansfield Park*, to Box Hill in *Emma*, to Lyme Regis in *Persuasion* – are always on the agenda for Austen's friendship groups, though when they happen (if they happen) they often end in tears.

Friendship groups in Austen tend to have a limited life-span; they are too big and unwieldy, too lively and heterogeneous to survive. The cliques in her fiction are often narcissistically thrilled at their own existence, but something normally happens to shatter the group's confidence in its own inseparability. Sir Thomas Bertram's return in *Mansfield Park* permanently disperses the excitable young clique who had made his home into their own unofficial headquarters. In *Emma*, the disastrously bad-tempered expedition to Box Hill seems to test one version of Highbury's elite friendship group – the 'chosen and the best' (*E*: 19) – to destruction.

As Austen's novels move towards their conclusions, an interlude of social hyperactivity will run its course, the clique's members will be released from its collective embrace as from a brief craze or obsession, and all those extraneous and unwanted friends – all the Isabella Thorpes and Mrs Eltons – will melt away. Normally it is the marriage of the novel's heroine that formally tidies things up, slims things down, re-establishes propriety and places the antics of the friendship group firmly in the past. Marriage, in Austen, draws a decorous but emphatic line under a period of 'general friendship' (*E*: 346) – that is, of the kind of promiscuous sociability that Emma Woodhouse so deplores in Mr Weston. The final pages of *Sense and Sensibility* witness a streamlining and consolidation of an intimate social world around Elinor, Marianne, Edward Ferrars and Colonel Brandon. *Emma*, likewise, seems relieved to be able to focus in the end on a 'small band of true friends' (*E*: 528) at Hartfield, with the days of balls and excursions firmly in the past.

But it is not always enough in Austen for friendship simply to come to an end or for an unmanageable friendship group to be disbanded. What was experienced as friendship in her writings is often re-classified, retrospectively, as never having been a true friendship in the first place. When Catherine Morland parts company from Isabella Thorpe, for example, we're not meant to mourn the demise of a friendship but rather to welcome the realization that this was only ever a pseudo-friendship, a sorry imitation of the real thing. The slow estrangement between Emma Woodhouse and Harriet Smith tells a similar story of friendship not just cancelled but annulled. Emma, as Knightley gravely informs her, has been 'no friend to Harriet Smith' (*E*: 66).

One lesson to be derived from these retroactively cancelled friendships is that, to quote Mrs Smith's plaintive words in *Persuasion*, 'There is so little real friendship in the world!' (*P*: 169). But what makes friendship so elusive and rare in Austen? Its customary activities – talking, walking, playing, dancing, music, eating, drinking, visiting, travelling, exchanging letters and **gifts** – are not exactly rare in her fiction. It would be unusual for a chapter to go by in Austen without some of these practices of friendship in evidence. What makes friendship seem troublingly scarce to a character such as Mrs Smith is not the absence of de facto evidence of friendly behaviour in her social world; rather it is a kind of lingering paranoia about the bona fides those who present themselves in the guise of friends. When there is no foolproof way of readily gauging sincerity or authenticity in the performance of friendly behaviour, we might need to steel ourselves for disappointment – or even betrayal. Added to this is the fact that friendship, unlike other key familial and emotional relations, cannot seek legal or institutional corroboration. There are no certificates or ceremonies, no legal contracts or religious rites, to confirm that person A is the friend of person B. Perhaps this very sense of fragility is what makes friendship so prone to overstate itself. The Dutchess in 'Henry and Eliza' professes lifelong friendship for the heroine the very moment she claps **eyes** on her. In *Northanger Abbey*, where Isabella Thorpe says that 'I carry my notions of friendship pretty high' (*NA*: 149) and insists that 'There is nothing I would not do for those who are really my friends' (*NA*: 33), the discourse of friendship is trafficked with such hyperbolic insincerity as always to be on the point of confessing its own groundlessness.

The unmasking and expulsion of false friends is something like a ritual pleasure in Austen's narratives. The bad friend's exclusion beyond the pale of a family-centred social circle provides a comforting fantasy that friendship can be triumphantly purged of any trace of inauthenticity. However, although the celebration of true friendship in Austen may seem to call for a regular and ongoing cull of unsuitable friends, her fiction does seem to have a certain lingering attachment to the false friends whom it so systematically disbars. From Isabella Thorpe to Lucy Steele to Mary Crawford, these are some of the most enliveningly problematic presences in the pages of Austen's fiction. Her storylines need them even if her moral frameworks don't. In the revolving-door logic of her friendship stories, Austen will always need a fresh supply of bad friends to excommunicate. It is revealing in this respect that the final line of dialogue in *Emma* is spoken not by one of the heroine's 'band of true friends' but by the dependably awful Mrs Elton. Chuntering resentfully about a wedding to which she has not been invited, the vicar's wife has been banished from the heroine's social circle but remains to the last a vivid citizen of *Emma*'s textual world. She has the last word, if not the last laugh. Whatever else we say about Austen's bad friends, they are always good friends of narrative.

G IS FOR GIFT

Many handsome gifts are given in Austen's fiction. In *Emma*, Frank Churchill gives **Jane** Fairfax a pianoforté. In *Sense and Sensibility*, Willoughby gives Marianne Dashwood a **horse** – or at least he tries to. 'Evelyn' is the exuberantly daft tale of a family who effectively give their entire life away to a complete stranger. The power of the gift, in her work, is complex and manifold. A gift is an announcement that you have a financial or material surplus that you can dispose of as you please. Gifts are freely given but place obligations of gratitude on those who receive them. Gifts also have the power to make stories happen, to open and close narratives. The gifted pianoforté is the talk of the town in *Emma*. The Bertrams' gift of an upbringing to Fanny Price initiates the story of *Mansfield Park*, while Colonel Brandon's gift of a living to Edward Ferrars helps to bring the tangled plot of *Sense and Sensibility* to a satisfying conclusion. Not that gifts in Austen are always quite so extravagant or decisive. In a novel such as *Emma*, the steady flow of modest and un-newsworthy presents and donations – chiefly of food – that circulates through Highbury testifies to a spirit of neighbourliness, generosity and **kindness** that her work evidently champions. But the gift is never a panacea or an ideal. Often, the gift in Austen is a problem – indeed, a double problem. First, because an individual gift, when ill-timed or ill-chosen, can pose difficulties for the recipient that are seemingly in excess of any pleasure or value derived from the item itself. Second, because the gift – and here Austen's work aligns with that of many thinkers who have pondered this issue (see Derrida 1992) – is a paradoxical entity. What makes a gift a gift is that it is gratuitous – it is freely given with no expectation of reciprocation or repayment. But it is difficult to imagine a practice of gift-giving that would not involve some form of quid pro quo, whether in the form of a gift in return, or the expression of gratitude, or even the symbolic repayment the giver gives themselves in seeing themselves as good and generous. If we always 'pay' in some way for the gifts that we receive, then we have to ask whether they were ever really gifts in the first place. Such questions are powerfully raised by Austen's narratives of donation, in which heroines from Marianne Dashwood to Fanny Price to Jane Fairfax have to reckon with the question of how to 'pay' for the fine gifts that are bestowed on them.

Gifts in Austen tend to flow from the powerful to the less powerful – from the rich to the **poor**, from men to women – and for this reason the trajectory of gift-giving in an Austen novel can provide a handy map of power-relations in its social worlds. A gift such as the bushel of apples donated by Mr Knightley to Miss Bates in *Emma* is an object whose journey from giver to receiver marks out a relationship in which power is disguised as largesse and subordinacy is articulated as gratitude. A gift is an object but also a message – one that is designed to convey affectionate regard for the needs, desires and preferences of the recipient but also to proclaim the giver's power to give. In *Sense and Sensibility*, when the Dashwoods arrive at Barton Cottage, their landlord Sir John Middleton sends them garden stuff, fruit and game, insists on taking care of their **letters** and sends them his newspaper every day. Who wouldn't be grateful for such easy-going munificence? Sir John seems to be a godsend for the Dashwoods, his open-handed generosity such a welcome change from the appallingly selfish behaviour of the relatives whom Austen's heroines have left behind in Sussex. The world would surely be a better place if there were more Sir Johns in it and fewer John and Fanny Dashwoods. However, it is far from easy to be on the receiving end of the kind of scattergun goodwill that emanates from Barton Park. Even a benefactor as welcoming and carelessly bountiful as Sir John expects a quid pro quo for his generosity. In return for the flow of gifts from Barton Park to Barton Cottage, Elinor and Marianne find themselves obliged to make themselves socially available to Sir John and his circle. At numerous **dances**, parties and get-togethers, Austen's refined heroines pay for his generosity with their privacy, offering themselves up to the Barton Park social circle as subjects of gossip, objects of speculation and targets of persistent, teasing curiosity about their personal lives. Or, to put it another way, the Dashwood sisters, like many women in Austen, repeatedly find that their private emotional lives have been objectified as gossip-narratives and 'gifted' to an entire community of prurient storytellers.

As they struggle with Sir John's insensitive and self-advertising generosity, the Dashwood sisters find themselves in a position where any deviation from the cultural norms of Barton Park looks like ingratitude. A sharper and more sustained version of the same predicament is undergone by Fanny Price in *Mansfield Park*, a heroine who, as Linda Zionkowski puts it, is a 'perpetual recipient' (2016: 153), defined – even deluged – by gifts that range from trivial cast-offs to incalculably valuable experiences. Often, presents are what *Mansfield Park*'s heroine receives instead of affection. Her cousins Maria and Julia offload 'some of their least valued toys' (*MP*: 15) on Fanny, while Tom Bertram – who 'made her some very pretty presents, and laughed at her' (*MP*: 20) – makes generosity and derision aspects of the same gesture. Despite the cruelty and indifference of her cousins, when Fanny contemplates their presents she finds herself 'bewildered as to the amount of the debt which all these kind remembrances produced' (*MP*: 179–80). As she gratefully surveys the 'present[s] upon present[s]' (*MP*: 179) that she has accumulated during her time at Mansfield – old toys, work-boxes, netboxes – Fanny is not simply curating worthless bric-a-brac but surveying evidence of the most lavish gift of all: the gift of an extraordinarily privileged upbringing.

The extent to which Fanny's identity has been constructed by gifts is underlined when she appears at the ball thrown in her honour by Sir Thomas. Fanny makes her entrance at this event wearing a gold necklace ostensibly from Mary Crawford (but actually from Henry Crawford), a gold chain from Edmund, an amber cross from her brother William and a white dress from Sir Thomas. In a scene where Fanny comes into her own as an autonomous adult, her social identity seems to be the sum of the fine gifts she has received from **friends** and family.

Whether Fanny has ever been sufficiently grateful for the gifts that have shaped her identity is the subject of ongoing disagreement in the Bertram household. Her beloved Edmund has no doubt that Fanny has 'a grateful heart' (*MP*: 30) while her spiteful nemesis Mrs Norris paints her as a monster of 'obstinacy and ingratitude' (*MP*: 176). Sir Thomas, usually detached in his Olympian way from such controversies, will come down on Mrs Norris's side of the argument when Fanny flatly refuses Henry Crawford's proposal of marriage. For Sir Thomas, Crawford's proposal is a wonderful gift – a timely solution to all sorts of problems – that his niece would be recklessly ungrateful to refuse.

Gifts can be cruel in their generosity. The pianoforté secretly gifted by Frank Churchill to Jane Fairfax is a case in point. A symbol of his devotion to Jane, the instrument is a sign of his capacity for mischief – an awkwardly extravagant addition to the already difficult burden of secrecy under which his fiancée labours. As Zionkowksi points out, nothing creates as much discussion and disagreement in *Emma* as gifts (2016: 180). The arrival of the pianoforté sparks off an interlude of intense speculation – not so much a whodunit as a who-gave-it in which the proliferation of suspects (Colonel

Campbell, Mr Knightley, Mrs Dixon, Mr Dixon) enables the true donor to hide in plain sight. In its vitalizing impact on local gossip, the pianoforté is thus a gift not only to Jane but to the neighbourhood at large. The Highbury poor need their food but the Highbury gossips need their talking points.

Whereas most of the presents that circulate in *Emma* are of food – a fine goose, say, or a hind-quarter of pork – a musical instrument is a luxury present that meets cultural rather than material needs. The pianoforté meets Jane's need for a means of artistic expression, and Highbury's need for something to chatter about. What is more, the very name of the gift – *piano* (soft/quiet), *forte* (strong/loud) – is a veritable gift of meaning to Austen's readers. The name is suggestive of the contrast between *piano* Jane's demure reticence and *forte* Frank's upbeat sociability – and indeed the contrast between the hushed-up question of the donor's identity and the voluble speculation that the instrument's arrival will provoke in Highbury. You have to hope that the instrument will give as much pleasure to Jane as the coup of its arrival has given to Frank.

Whether they depict ostentatious gift-givers like Sir John Middleton or incognito male donors such as Henry Crawford and Frank Churchill, Austen's narratives of donation often suggest that there is a kind of circularity in gift-giving. What might look like a lavish act of generosity often turns out to be another instance in which a patriarchal system gifts power and pleasure to itself. Some of Austen's most revealing insights into this aspect of gift-giving are obtained when it goes wrong in some way – when the gift is not given or not accepted. There are two notable instances in her work of a horse that is, as it were, half-given, from a man to a woman. In *Mansfield Park*, a mare is 'given' by Edmund to Fanny and then soon after effectively re-given to Mary Crawford. We only need to follow this horse's journey to trace the trajectories of affection and desire that link Edmund to Fanny and Mary. In *Sense and Sensibility*, Willoughby gives Marianne a horse, Queen Mab, that she cannot accept. To accept the horse, the Dashwoods would need a stable, and a groom, who would in turn need his own horse. Willoughby cannot give this gift because the Dashwoods cannot receive what they don't already have. This ungiven horse is an odd kind of virtual gift or ungiven gift, one that makes Willoughby seem generous without having given anything and obliges Marianne to be beholden to him without actually receiving anything.

In its dazzling generosity, the gift in Austen both highlights and disguises a relationship in which to accept a gift is to accept that you belong, in some sense, to the donor. The gift of the horse is designed to make Marianne belong to Willoughby, just as the gift of the gold necklace is designed to link

Fanny Price permanently to Henry Crawford. But gifts – and the coercive designs that underlie them – can be rejected. It's possible, though not easy, to say **no**. In a world where women are deluged by presents, the moment when Jane Fairfax refuses to accept Emma's gift of arrowroot stands out as a remarkable assertion of autonomy. Jane won't let her relationship with Austen's heroine be defined by a debt of gratitude. Emma can't donate her way into intimacy with Jane or use her as a short-cut to moral rehabilitation after the disgrace of Box Hill. Austen's heroines are inundated by – and in some ways constructed as – gifts, but Jane makes an emphatic declaration of independence when she stoutly refuses a gift that seeks to define her.

H IS FOR HORSE

Horses are so ubiquitous in Austen, and journeys on horseback or in horse-drawn carriages such a familiar part of social experience in her worlds, that it becomes easy not to notice the actual creatures when they appear in her novels. Indeed, in expressions such as 'the carriage turned' (*PP*: 191), 'the carriage drove off' (*MP*: 94) or 'the carriage returned' (*E*: 347), Austen's evocations of horse-powered motion frequently erase the animals that are doing the moving, the driving and the returning. But once we notice those little horse-shaped gaps in Austen's wording we can begin to appreciate the extent to which her novels might be described as horse-powered narratives. Horse-power refers in this context to the physical power of the four-legged beasts to carry riders, pull carriages, convey loads and traverse distances beyond the scope of the foot-traveller. There is an active and diverse pedestrian culture in Austen, to be sure, but it is the horse that grants her characters – and by extension her fiction – access to a world outside the country village and its immediate environs. Horses also carry or embody a considerable amount of symbolic power in the world of her fiction. Beyond their practical function as modes of transport, fine horses and carriages in Austen's world are designed to attract deferential attention by making a mobile spectacle of their owners' wealth and status. Horse-drawn carriages – and their privileged, elevated occupants – represent the class system on wheels.

Associated with status, elevation and mobility, horse-power in Austen is a distinctive expression and extension of the privileges enjoyed by men in the society of her time. Men's comings and goings in her fiction – often beyond the immediate horizons of the storyline – are enabled by their ready access to horses. In *Emma*, this kind of masculine mobility can be a matter of routine business, as in the case of Robert Martin's weekly rides to Kingston, or it can be a seemingly spur-of-the-moment impulse, as when Frank Churchill sends for a chaise to take him to London for a haircut. Either way, men's access to horses is a passport to a wider world of business, sociability and off-stage plotting outside of the comparatively static heroine's sphere of everyday experience. From the vantage-point of that more restricted female space, the departures and comebacks of male horse-riders are often monitored with keen interest. Twice in *Sense and Sensibility* an as-yet-unidentified man on horseback is eagerly observed by Austen's heroine Elinor Dashwood as he trots into her field of vision (*SS*: 99–100, 405–6). Captured in these moments of watchful uncertainty is a gendered experience of space, movement and power in a social world where elegantly immobilized women wait for privileged, elevated men to ride into their lives, bringing with them the exhilarating prospect of transformative motion. However, the fact that in both cases the unknown horseman turns out to be Edward Ferrars – Austen's most pallidly underdeveloped male love interest – suggests that Austen is not *too* naively invested in the figure of the male equestrian saviour.

Overwhelmingly, if not exclusively, it is Austen's flawed male characters who exhibit an interest in an equestrian culture where ownership and mastery of horses signifies money, speed, accomplishment and prowess in a sharply competitive world. Whether they are obsessed with buying and selling horses (like John Thorpe in *Northanger Abbey*), or betting on horse races (like Tom Bertram in *Mansfield Park*) or fox-hunting (like Lord Osborne in *The Watsons*), Austen's horse-fixated men are in the grip of an obsession to which her fiction is studiedly immune. Austen's narratives will never give us a ring-side seat at scenes of horse-trading or horse-racing or fox-hunting but this 'gap' in her work is experienced not as limitation or demoralizing exclusion but rather with a sense of relief. Not simply because the world of horses is a dangerous world – Henry Hervey in 'Lesley Castle' dies after being thrown from his horse while Tom Bertram narrowly escapes with his life after his equestrian **accident** – but because it's *boring* in its dangerousness. There is no more deadly conversation-stopper in Austen than talk of horses, and it's hard not to suspect that Austen takes a certain vindictive pleasure in making men such as Hervey and Bertram victims of their most tedious hobby.

The point at which men in Austen start talking about horses is often the point at which women stop listening. Austen's family **friend** William-Glanvill Evelyn, who 'all his life thought more of Horses than of anything else' (*L*: 49), is one representative of male equestrian monomania in her world. There is no question that, as Jillian Heydt-Stevenson has persuasively demonstrated, Austen's fiction 'humorously mines the sexual nuances of all things equestrian' (2005: 117), not least in the ribald puns around 'riding' in *Mansfield Park*. But it is worth noticing how equestrian obsessions are equated with simple ineptitude in the field of conversation and courtship. Approaching Fanny at what is the first ball she has ever attended, Tom Bertram decides that this will be a good moment to launch into a detailed account of a sick horse (*MP*: 139).

Of all Austen's male equestrian obsessives, the most relentless – and the most conversationally incompetent – is John Thorpe in *Northanger Abbey*. '[H]is equipage was altogether the most complete of its kind in England' – the narrator reports, in a calculatedly flat rendering of Thorpe's breathless hyperbole – 'his carriage the neatest, his horse the best goer, and himself the best coachman' (*NA*: 61). When a man can talk of nothing but horses, then a conversation about what should be the great symbol of mobility has nowhere to go except the dead-end of mind-numbingly insistent overstatement. A character whose only real talent is for bluster and exaggeration, Thorpe excels himself when he boasts to Catherine Morland of owning a horse that '*cannot* go less than ten miles an hour' (*NA*: 40). The horse in question is a curious hybrid of fact and fantasy. A horse that gets overheated en route from Tetbury to **Bath** seems real enough, but one that cannot go below ten miles per hour deserves a place alongside Pegasus in the stable of fabulous quadrupeds. Austen is an impeccably realistic novelist but some of the most outlandish exaggerations in her fictions are voiced when men talk about horses.

There is a tendency among Austen's men to make horses the measure of their own imagined social significance. No one in her fiction is more lavishly endowed with horses and horse-drawn vehicles than Mr Clifford, the Bath gentleman and hero of an unfinished fragment from her childhood: '[He] had a Coach, a Chariot, a Chaise, a Landeau, a Landeaulet, a Phaeton, a Gig, a Whisky, an italian Chair, a Buggy, a Curricle and a wheelbarrow. He had likewise an amazing fine stud of Horses. To my knowledge he had six Greys, 4 Bays, eight Blacks and a poney' ('Memoirs of Mr Clifford', *J*: 51). This preposterously lavish inventory of horses and carriages is seemingly testament to Clifford's tremendous mobility, but Austen's hero gets nowhere in the course of this fragmentary tale, most of which he spends resting up somewhere between Bath and London. The comic impact of this short piece derives from the gap between Clifford's symbolic and real horse-power – between the commanding power and dynamism proclaimed by his magnificent stable and the feeble sluggishness of his unfinished, slow-motion journey to the capital.

Austen is always studiously unimpressed by those who want to make a spectacle of their own horse-power. Repeat offenders in this regard are the Eltons in *Emma*. Mrs Elton peppers her conversation with references to her rich brother-in-law and his barouche-landau (*E*: 295, 306, 372), while her clergyman husband cannot resist making boastful reference to their horse and carriage (*E*: 348). The point about the barouche-landau or the carriage is not so much the physical travel they might enable as the social journey that they can evidence – a glorious upward journey, as the Eltons see it, through the higher ranks of respectable provincial England. For all that we are encouraged to laugh at the Eltons' fixation on the equestrian trappings of social privilege, there's no doubt that upward mobility in Austen is frequently experienced in and through horse-drawn vehicles. For Austen heroines from a relatively humble background – Catherine Morland, Fanny Price – the horse-drawn carriage becomes a kind of viewing platform on wheels from which they can enjoy a newly privileged vantage-point on the English countryside as an unfolding, picturesque spectacle rather than a site of productivity or a scene of labour (*NA*: 159–60; *MP*: 94–7). Downward mobility, it has to be said, is also experienced through changing relationships with horse-drawn vehicles. Catherine Morland is conveyed from Bath to Northanger Abbey in all the grandeur of a chaise and four, and sent ignominiously back home in a mere 'hack post-chaise' (*NA*: 241).

Horse-powered journeys in Austen often begin with a flurry of debate about the mode of travel and – if carriages are being used – about who will sit with whom. In *Pride and Prejudice*, the question of whether **Jane** Bennet should make the three-mile journey from Longbourn to Netherfield on horseback or via horse-drawn carriage is freighted with consequence. This will be the most important journey of her life, one that – if Mrs Bennet has her way – will turn out to be a one-way journey into membership of the Bingley family. If Jane had travelled by carriage – that is, if she hadn't fallen ill after being exposed to the elements on horseback – would she have ended up marrying Bingley? And would Elizabeth, who follows to tend to the ailing horsewoman, have ended up marrying Mr Darcy? It's hard to say; but what we can say is that Mrs Bennet's strategic under-playing of her family's own horse-power provides significant impetus for her eldest daughter's journey towards happiness and security.

Carriage rides in Austen can create self-contained dramas that are heightened for the duration of the journey. When groups of friends embark on carriage journeys, there is often a frantic interlude of musical chairs as travellers vie to achieve advantageous positions. In *Mansfield Park*, Henry Crawford uses the expedition to Sotherton, expertly, to manage his flirtation with Maria and Julia Bertram, whom he rotates in the keenly sought-after position next to him on the barouche-box. Such jockeying for position is as revealing in its own way as the question of who **dances** with whom at a ball – except that the carriage can render women more vulnerable and isolated than the dancefloor. Carriage rides for Austen's women can be hypnotically boring and claustrophobically unpleasant experiences. Frequently, unwanted suitors use horse-drawn vehicles to isolate and control her heroines. In *Emma* the heroine has the wretched luck of finding herself alone with Mr Elton in John Knightley's carriage on the ride home from Randalls as he makes a wine-soaked declaration of love. In *Northanger Abbey*, John Thorpe uses excursions to Claverton Down and to Blaize Castle to make a horse-powered display of control over Catherine's position, direction and destination.

Austen's writings don't get us particularly close to the snorting, stamping physicality of horses, and she leaves us in no doubt that horses are fairly low on the list of subjects that command her impassioned interest. However, even though her fiction doesn't centre on horses, she wants us to notice when they are not there. The reduced circumstances of the Dashwoods in *Sense and Sensibility*, for example, are indicated by the fact that they keep no horse – and they don't have the space or resources to accept the **gift** of one from Willoughby. But horselessness in Austen is not necessarily a sign of indigence. In *Emma*, Mr Knightley keeps no carriage horses of his own even though we can assume that, as the richest person in the neighbourhood, he could easily afford to do so (*E*: 230). It's a detail that reflects well on Knightley's unflashy demeanour. Whereas the hero of 'Mr Clifford' seeks to make his 'amazing fine stud of Horses' the sign and measure of his superior social standing, the most impressive horses in *Emma* are the ones that the hero doesn't own.

I IS FOR ILLNESS

'A sick chamber', says Anne Elliot in *Persuasion*, 'may often furnish the worth of volumes' (*P*: 169). These words are inspired by Anne's assumption that a professional care-giver such as Nurse Rooke will witness edifying scenes of 'heroism, fortitude, patience, resignation' (*P*: 169) in the course of her duties in the sickroom. Austen, it has to be said, doesn't share her heroine's somewhat high-minded idealization of the experience of illness and the practices of care and recovery, and she certainly doesn't go to the sickroom in search of moral uplift. But she does nevertheless find abundant narrative possibilities in sickness. '[I]llness among family and **friends**' (2012: 244), as John Mullan remarks, is the single most persistent preoccupation of her **letters**. Her fiction, meanwhile, consistently engages with and is shaped by the maladies of its characters – from seemingly trivial ailments (such as the sore throat that prevents Harriet Smith from attending the party at Randalls in *Emma*) to life-threatening fevers (such as the one experienced by Marianne Dashwood in *Sense and Sensibility*).

The references to health and illness that provide so much of the anecdotal substance of Austen's letters are often laced with droll scepticism. Writing from Lyme, she comments on how 'fever and indisposition' have become 'all the fashion' in the seaside town (*L*: 96). One acquaintance, Harriet Bridges, is 'determined never to be well' and 'likes her spasms & nervousness & the consequence they give her, better than anything else' (*L*: 240). Nor are her family exempt from this kind of ironic exasperation at habitual unwellness. 'Dearest Henry!', she writes of her brother, 'What a turn he has for being ill!' (*L*: 264). Precisely the same phrase will be used by Mrs Parker in *Sanditon* when she laments that the medical obsessions of Susan and Diana Parker have given their hypochondriac brother Arthur 'such a turn for being ill' (*LM*: 165). Austen's writings don't always exhibit a tremendous amount of imaginative solidarity with their ailing characters. As John Wiltshire points out, Austen never really evokes illness from the inside; she doesn't get us close to the first-person experience of what it feels like to be queasily, painfully unwell. The sick person in her writings is often glimpsed, rather, from the perspective of a non-ill observer who focuses on the 'performance' (Wiltshire 1992: 20) of illness. 'Performance' in this context can refer to illnesses whose symptoms are exaggerated or even imagined (there are plenty of hypochondriacs in Austen), but it can also be understood in a more extended sense as referring to the way illness is reported, talked about, interpreted and catered for. Whatever its debilitating or immobilizing effects on the individual, illness has a lively symbolic and discursive existence in Austen's social worlds – even to the extent, in *Sanditon*, of forming the basis of an entire community.

When Austen's characters meet they often find conversational common ground in questions of health and illness. In *Emma*, the perceived **risk** of illness frames Mr Woodhouse's understanding of social experience in his family circle. A typical exchange with Isabella Knightley covers sore throats, biliousness, colds, influenza, headaches and palpitations in just a couple of pages (*E*: 109–11), much to the irritation of John Knightley, who bristles at his wife's habit of 'doctoring and coddling yourself and the **children**' (*E*: 111). John Knightley's implied logic seems to be that anyone who can talk so enthusiastically about illness can't be all that ill – unless you would regard unhealthy fear of and fascination with illness as itself amounting to a kind of meta-illness, one that perhaps deserves more sympathetic attention than Emma's no-nonsense brother-in-law is prepared to give it.

An important distinction in Austen is between those who use illness to seek attention and those who take refuge in illness from publicity and exposure. In *Emma*, **Jane** Fairfax's uncertain health provides an instructive study in the ways the 'performance' of illness cannot be reduced to hypochondria or malingering. Reports that Jane has uncertain pulmonary health circulate widely in Highbury; medical gossip is one way in which the neighbourhood lays siege to her privacy. But Jane's uncertain health also secures her from unwanted visitors (not least from Emma herself, at one stage) and provides her with at least some cover during her months of distress, anxiety and vulnerability in the Bates household. Illness is hardly an enviable or empowering state for Jane, then, but it does serve as an important element of her medium-term survival strategy during her ordeal of secrecy and isolation at Highbury. As with Jane Fairfax in *Emma* so with Marianne Dashwood in *Sense and Sensibility*, who finds in the distress of illness and indisposition an emergency exit from the claustrophobic spaces of mandatory sociability. A 'turn for being ill' gives these Austen heroines a precious alibi, a respectable way of not having to be energetically, irrepressibly present in society.

But illness, as various readers have noted, can also function to restrict and discipline Austen's characters (see: Gorman 1993: 111–13; Tanner 2007: 81–5). At times, Austen's fiction comes close to implying, in a moralistic vein, that illness is good for you. Tom Bertram in *Mansfield Park*, who becomes dangerously ill with putrid fever after a fall from his **horse**, is described after his recovery as being 'the better for ever for his illness' (*MP*: 534). In the moral world of this novel, illness is both the punishment for Tom's delinquent behaviour and the agent of his permanent rehabilitation. Marianne in *Sense and Sensibility* also seems to have illness to thank for her personal reformation. Throughout the novel, her turbulent inner life finds expression through symptoms of disturbed health – sleeplessness, tearfulness, 'head-aches, low spirits, and over fatigues' (*SS*: 184). What is more, her level-headed sister Elinor suspects that Marianne may be a little too susceptible to the dark glamour of illness – the 'flushed cheek, hollow **eye**, and quick pulse of a fever' (*SS*: 46). When Marianne does become gravely ill – she contracts a life-threatening fever at the Palmers' house after getting wet on a series of solitary twilight walks – her condition is seen as a product of a pattern of risky behaviour that long preceded those walks. Her illness is frighteningly real but it also symbolically confirms the moral diagnosis the novel wants to impart – namely, that Marianne has already been ill for as long as she has been a naively wholehearted devotee of the cult of sensibility. An uncompromisingly idealistic commitment to art, beauty and nature has left Marianne dangerously disengaged from the shared commonsense values of the prosaic and non-sublime world. A dangerous bout of illness 'cures' her of the disease of excess sensibility by manifesting its psychological symptoms as physical ones from which she can make a full recovery into clear-eyed moral health.

Austen's final, unfinished novel, *Sanditon*, is a satirical thought experiment about illness not as an interruption to ordinary living but as a freely chosen way of life. Via its eminently healthy and level-headed heroine Charlotte Heywood, this text casts a droll diagnostic eye over the varieties of imagined illness exhibited by the eccentrics who converge at a sea-side health resort where they can play at sickness and invalidism. At stake in this text is the question of whether we can differentiate between sham or imagined illness on the one hand and the real thing on the other. Such delicate questions of interpretation are posed here in the context of a broader investigation of the relations between illness, privilege and social status. As in her representations of **Bath**, Austen's imagination is stirred by the curious continuity between illness, indulgence and privileged leisure. Not everyone is lucky enough to have a life of invalidism. If the Heywoods had had fewer children and a bit more disposable income, they might have enjoyed the luxuries of 'gout and a winter at Bath' (*LM*: 149). Poor health, in other words, is a perk of affluence – a lifestyle choice in which the idle rich can experience their own unproductivity as a pitiable affliction rather than an enviable luxury. It is Lady Denham who comes closest to acknowledging the class hierarchies that underpin experiences of health and illness in Sanditon: 'I beseech you Mr Parker, no doctors here', she says. 'It would only be encouraging our **servants** and the **poor** to fancy themselves ill' (*LM*: 171). In this pre-emptive strike against the democratization of illness, the grande dame of Sanditon more or less admits that poor health should be available only to those with the means to pay.

Anyone can fall ill, but in Austen's social worlds access to the status of invalidism is a function of pre-existing power relations. Even as her fiction encourages a coolly sceptical view of 'performed' illness, however, it can be sceptical about its own diagnostic scepticism. Relations between privilege and real/imagined illness are explored in a notably surprising way in Austen's depiction of Mrs Churchill in *Emma*. Frank Churchill's fearsome aunt is an off-stage character whose unpopularity is compounded by the suspicion that her frequent illnesses 'never occurred but for her own convenience' (*E*: 279). It is a measure of Mrs Churchill's dislikeability that the ordinarily genial Mr Weston struggles to find a good word to say about his sister-in-law. He describes one of her episodes of illness as 'all nothing of course' (*E*: 328) but insists elsewhere that 'I never allow myself to speak ill of her' (*E*: 130) and that 'I would not speak ill of her' (*E*: 332). Weston repeatedly declares himself reluctant to speak ill of the ill, even if he openly suspects that the illness, in Mrs Churchill's case, may be all talk. Revealingly amplified in his conflicted commentary on his sister-in-law's health is the *ill* in Churchill – as though illness might, after all, be a genuinely intrinsic part of her identity rather than a deplorable ruse that we can all see through. In the event, Mrs Churchill's death – an extraordinarily rare outcome in an Austen novel, many of whose characters are afflicted by illness but almost none of whom die – will acquit her 'of all the fancifulness, and all the selfishness of imaginary complaints' (*E*: 422). All the fancifulness and the selfishness, in other words, belong to those who were heartless enough to suspect that Mrs Churchill was faking it.

Austen's fiction does not pretend to have any definitive answer to the imponderable conundrum of where 'subjective' illness ends and 'objective' illness begins, and the case of Mrs Churchill in *Emma* elegantly ambushes those readers who believe they have arrived at secure medical – and indeed moral – distinctions between imagined ailments and the real thing. Illness, in her novels, is always open to a range of physiological, symbolic and political readings. A medical disorder can bring someone's life to a standstill but it keeps conversation open and narrative moving. When the possibilities for diagnostic storytelling are so endless, it would be unhealthy to foreclose them, even if the patient in question is deceased.

J IS FOR JANE

Austen is one of those writers with whom many readers like to feel they are on first-name terms. The English critic George Saintsbury coined the term 'Janite' as an affectionate nickname for Austen devotees in his introduction to an 1894 edition of *Pride and Prejudice*, and the term would be adapted and popularized by Rudyard Kipling in a short story about a secret society of Austen admirers in the ranks of the British military. Kipling's story, 'The Janeites' (1926), implies a cult (Janeism) and an object of devotion (Jane). The cult has always had its refuseniks. As early as 1905 Henry James (mischievously described by one character in 'The Janeites' as Austen's only son) was bemoaning the publishing industry for constructing a sentimental and saleable myth of 'their "dear", our dear, everybody's dear, Jane' (1984: 118). His protests have been ineffective. Austen's posthumous celebrity is greater than ever in the twenty-first century – indeed, it is such a thriving branch of the UK heritage industry that the reception of her life and works has become a significant topic of scholarly interest in its own right. The study of Jane Austen has now broadened to include the study of 'Jane Austen' – a literary celebrity and cultural phenomenon who has enjoyed a hectic and diverse afterlife, in biographies and critical studies, in unofficial sequels and re-imaginings, and in television and film adaptations (Lynch 2000; Johnson 2012; Looser 2017). The appearance of Austen's face on a British banknote on the 200th anniversary of her death only confirmed the enduringly powerful currency, in both senses of the word, of her identity. When the banknote was issued a UK politician attracted widespread derision by referring to Austen as one of the country's 'greatest living authors', but let's be charitable and concede that the gaffe contains a grain of truth – not many authors live on more vividly in the collective imagination than Austen.

If we are looking for a moment when Jane Austen, the historical person, became 'Jane', the iconic literary figure, then we could point to the memoirs and recollections produced by her brother Henry (1818), her nieces Anna Lefroy (1864) and Caroline Austen (1867), and her nephew James Edward Austen-Leigh (1871). The 'dear Aunt Jane' depicted in these fond family recollections is an idealized, indeed 'Faultless' (Henry Austen in Austen-Leigh [2002]: 139) creature – gentle, devout, loving, virtuous and good with **children**, but with none of the formidable intelligence or satirical sharpness of her writings. The 'Aunt Jane' persona has not lost its hold on those who crave a sense of a reassuring familial intimacy with their favourite author (Looser 2017: 5–10) even if many modern readers have been drawn to robustly unsentimental versions of the author as social malcontent and political radical. Without weighing in on the debate about which version of the author's reputation counts as the 'real' Jane Austen, it's possible to trace the mythologization of 'Jane' even further back into Austen's own fictional writings. None of Austen's protagonists shares her first name, but Janes are sprinkled through her fiction. There is Jane Bennet in *Pride and Prejudice* and Jane Fairfax in *Emma*. There is the **young** widow Miss Jane in 'A Collection of Letters', who decides not to take the names either of her late husband or of her late father and makes a point of 'bearing only my Christian one' (*J*: 196). There is the amiable but put-upon Janetta McDonald in 'Love and Freindship'. In *The Watsons* there is the heroine's sister-in-law Jane Watson, a 'pert and conceited' (*LM*: 119) attorney's daughter, pleased with her own fashionability, and easy to dislike. The most tellingly inconspicuous Jane in Jane Austen is the 'Mrs Jane Fisher' whose name appears in the unexciting list of subscribers to Mrs Whitby's library in *Sanditon* (*LM*: 166). Are there any continuities between these various Janes in Jane Austen's work? Critics who have pondered this question argue that the common denominators between Jane's Janes begin and end with the name that they share (Lane 2002: 68; Doody 2016: 167). It would be nice to believe that we could catch Austen in the act of performing Hitchcock-like cameos in her own novels and stories, but her first name is one that she seems to use in unsystematic, unpredictably diverse and decidedly non-autobiographical ways. Her biographer, Park Honan, has even hinted that if we are looking for self-portraits in Austen then we should look not to her Janes but to her Emmas – a name she uses 'with such affection that her parents might have wondered why they called her Jane' (1987: 72).

Before we abandon all hope of discerning some trace of Jane Austen in her fictional Janes, however, it might be worth narrowing our focus to the two most fully realized among them, the Janes of *Pride and Prejudice* and *Emma*. Promisingly, Jane Bennet and Jane Fairfax share more than a first name. They are both characterized by sweetness, intelligence and elegance (indeed, they are both to a notable extent more elegant than the domestic circumstances in which they find themselves). Their stories are marked by periods of **illness** and uncertainty, ordeals that they endure with uncomplaining patience that is rewarded when they are partnered with affluent, sociable, fun-loving men who like to **dance**. And both of them *might* have been the protagonists of their respective novels. The romance between Jane Bennet and Bingley shapes up, in the novel's early chapters, to be the central story of *Pride and Prejudice*, while Jane Fairfax's secret relationship with Frank Churchill could easily have been the subject of a novel in its own right. W. J. Harvey has even made a case for Jane and Frank as the protagonists of what he calls the 'shadow novel-within-a-novel' (1967: 56) in *Emma*. Jane Bennet and Jane Fairfax thus seem to represent two versions of the same figure – the authorial namesake who is endowed with all sorts of enviable qualities but consigned to the tantalizingly off-centre position of shadow-heroine or nearly heroine.

There would be no reason for a first-time reader of *Pride and Prejudice* to suppose that the protagonist of the novel will be anyone but Jane Bennet. She is the eldest Bennet daughter, unmarried and by all accounts beautiful and accomplished – and with the arrival of an eligible bachelor in the neighbourhood she is poised to play the lead role in a courtship narrative. If Bingley is the 'single man' of the novel's almost oppressively famous opening sentence, then Jane Bennet is evidently the future 'wife' of whom he is 'in want' (*PP*: 3). As things turn out, however, the novel's opening is a subtle act of misdirection, and it's not long before Jane is yielding pride of place to Elizabeth. Just as Mr Collins 'had only to change from Jane to Elizabeth' (*PP*: 79) when he learns that the former is romantically unavailable, so the novel performs is its own pivot from the first to the second Bennet daughter. However, while Jane effectively ceases to exist for Mr Collins once she has been ruled out as a potential wife, Austen's text will continue to represent Jane's identity as intimately entangled with Elizabeth's. Such is the closeness between the two sisters that it can seem difficult for the novel to think of one without thinking of the other. Whenever Jane Bennet is mentioned in *Pride and Prejudice* there is a fair chance that Elizabeth will be mentioned in the same sentence. References to 'Jane and Elizabeth' (*PP*: 15, 67, 69, 126, 159, 243, 332, 346, 348, 427) – or, just once, 'Elizabeth and Jane' (*PP*: 359) – are laced through the text. The 'elder Miss Bennets' (*PP*: 254) figure in the novel as a sympathetic double act, thinking and feeling in tandem with one another, united by their intelligence and sensibility in a social world that is often short of both qualities.

Few characters in Austen excite more lavish admiration than Jane Bennet. The novel has hardly got underway when Bingley describes her as 'the most beautiful creature I ever beheld!' (*PP*: 12). He subsequently insists that he 'could not conceive an angel more beautiful' (*PP*: 18) and will never tire of enlarging on her 'perfections' (*PP*: 385) and on her 'excellent understanding, and super-excellent disposition' (*PP*: 385). Nor is Bingley the only cheerleader of Jane's perfections. Elizabeth will also praise Jane's 'angelic' (*PP*: 153) qualities, her 'most affectionate, generous heart' (*PP*: 209) and her 'loveliness and goodness' (*PP*: 209). Perfect, angelic, super-excellent and surpassingly beautiful – Austen hasn't done too badly by her namesake. But it is precisely this apparent perfection that makes Jane something of a problem for a novelist who doesn't quite know what to do with flawlessness. '[P]ictures of perfection', Austen famously writes to her niece Fanny Knight, 'make me sick & wicked' (*L*: 350). Jane Bennet's angelic flawlessness doesn't make people sick but it can test their patience. 'Of whom does Jane ever think ill?' (*PP*: 313), asks Elizabeth, conscious that her sister's only real flaw is an inability to see flaws in others. In her generous willingness to see the good in people, and in her gentle and undemonstrative flawlessness, Jane can seem like an outsider in this novel's imaginative world, an unsatirical and unsatirizable presence in a novel that is alive with satirical laughter.

You can see why Elizabeth so swiftly upstages Jane. The more spirited, opinionated, headstrong and playful of the two, Elizabeth provides much more for us in the way of page-by-page entertainment – sharp wisecracks, fearless opinions and bold **risk**-taking. Her overall story-arc – she has to recalibrate her ethical judgements, and, in so doing, become a new version of herself – is also more compellingly transformative than that of her sister. Characterized by calm, elegant stasis, Jane Bennet at the end of *Pride and Prejudice* is not so radically different from Jane Bennet at the beginning of the novel – perhaps because she is neither proud nor prejudiced. Given the nature of this contrast between the two sisters, it's perhaps unsurprising that as the story unfolds we will have opportunities to see Elizabeth without Jane but we don't tend to see Jane without Elizabeth. The novel admires Jane but it doesn't seem to want to spend too much time alone with her.

Whereas Jane Bennet is positioned as the potential heroine of *Pride and Prejudice*, there is no danger of us suspecting that Jane Fairfax might be the protagonist of *Emma*. The novel's primary focus on Emma Woodhouse is emphatically settled by its title and its first sentence, and we are ten chapters into the storyline before Jane is even mentioned. Revealingly, it is Emma herself who is the first person to name her directly. When the topic of Miss Bates's niece arises, our heroine declares that 'One is sick of the very name of Jane Fairfax' (*E*: 92). We've not even met Jane, and Emma has already had enough of her. What is it about Jane, we have to ask, that gets our heroine so riled up? The very fact that Highbury has discovered a topic of conversation that isn't Emma Woodhouse seems to be part of the problem for our heroine – a problem compounded by Jane's evident popularity. Mrs John Knightley refers to her as 'That sweet, amiable Jane Fairfax!' (*E*: 112), Mrs Elton as 'sweet Jane Fairfax' (*E*: 305) and Knightley as 'that sweet young woman' (*E*: 465). We don't hear much of Jane Fairfax's voice in *Emma* but her name is on everyone's lips, often doubled or even tripled: 'Jane, Jane, look' (*E*: 348); 'Jane, Jane, my dear Jane, where are you?' (*E*: 355); 'Jane, Jane, you will be a miserable creature' (*E*: 465). When Highbury's residents are not talking about Jane Fairfax, they are often eager to talk about the way people talk about Jane Fairfax. '"Jane," indeed!' (*E*: 481), says Frank Churchill, who even at his most expansively upbeat can't forgive Mrs Elton for her over-familiar habit of referring to his fiancée by her first name. Emma is equally scandalized by Mrs Elton's habit of bandying Jane's name around: '"Jane Fairfax and Jane Fairfax." Heavens!' (*E*: 306). Jane Fairfax is a name that becomes insistently audible even as its self-effacing owner takes refuge in subdued and self-contained privacy; it is constantly amplified and multiplied in the chatter of Highbury. 'Jane', in *Emma*, is both a screen concealing someone whom we never really get to know and an arrow or signpost that points with insistent publicity towards Highbury's most self-effacing resident.

The Janes of *Pride and Prejudice* and *Emma* are – ever so slightly – muffled and sidelined by the language in which they are affectionately idealized. A valuable insight into why they are so delicately marginalized is offered by Austen's tongue-in-cheek 'Plan of a Novel' (1816). Here, Austen provides a sketch of an impeccably virtuous heroine – 'faultless […] perfectly good, with much tenderness & sentiment, & not the least Wit' (*LM*: 226) – who is unable to reciprocate the overtures of friendship from a neighbour because the latter has 'a considerable degree of Wit' (*LM*: 227). The contrast between the faultless non-witty character and their witty counterpart will be familiar to anyone who has read *Pride and Prejudice* or *Emma*. In both texts, a sweet-natured, demure and seemingly faultless Jane is upstaged by a confidently witty counterpart – Elizabeth Bennet in one case, Emma Woodhouse in the other. The Janes of these novels are disqualified from starring roles by the very qualities of sweetness and virtue that might seem to mark them out as heroines, while Elizabeth Bennet and Emma Woodhouse achieve centrality precisely because of their un-Jane-like qualities.

Austen is never a transparently autobiographical writer. Jane Austen is not Jane Bennet or Jane Fairfax. But she does seem to be using idealized namesakes in *Pride and Prejudice* and *Emma*, with calculated playfulness,

K IS FOR KINDNESS

'Incline us Oh God!', says Austen, in one of the three prayers that she is known to have composed, '[...] to consider our fellow-creatures with kindness' (*LM*: 575). The Christian principles of charity and compassion that are warmly espoused by the author in this devotional text are often conspicuous by their absence in the world of her fiction, where an atmosphere of calculating selfishness, if not outright spite and cruelty, often seems to prevail. Christopher Ricks, in an essay on Austen and **children**, remarks that her writings 'expose cruelty [...] with such imaginative cogency as necessarily to recommend kindness, but they do not much show kindness in action' (1996: 100).

How do we account for the apparent invisibility of 'kindness in action' in Austen's worlds? One possibility is that, for Austen, there simply isn't enough kindness in the world, that in our dealings with each other we too easily and routinely fall short of what should be an easily achievable standard of human decency. What is more, the scarcity of kindness is compounded by its self-effacingness – kindness, when it does happen, doesn't make itself the centre of attention. When Anne Elliot makes a series of dutiful, low-key **visits** to the ailing, impoverished widow Mrs Smith in an unfashionable quarter of **Bath**, it is not in search of glory or renown. On the other hand, it could be that Austen's art secretly thrives on unkindness – that she needs the vivid unpleasantness of unkind characters and cruel behaviour as targets for satire and isn't above indulging in unkindness for laughs. Readers of her **letters** have occasionally professed to be shocked by the streak of cruel humour that they intermittently display. Nor can the novels always resist the pleasures of malice. In *Persuasion*, there is something astonishingly exorbitant about the energy with which Austen lampoons a deceased minor character – the 'troublesome, hopeless [...] stupid and unmanageable [...] thick-headed, unfeeling, unprofitable' (*P*: 54) Dick Musgrave – whose memory seems to have been summoned into the world of the novel principally as the object of cruel humour.

The unkindness that flares up sporadically in Austen's writerly voice is a disturbingly pervasive force in her social worlds. Often, it is secondary female characters – Eliza Williams and her daughter in *Sense and Sensibility*, Georgiana Darcy in *Pride and Prejudice*, Mrs Smith in *Persuasion* – who are most grievously affected by cruelty, usually at the hands of men. The ordeals of these victimized women provide a cautionary context for Austen's heroines as they begin to negotiate a new social landscape in which some **young** women find secure love and friendship while others are used and heartlessly discarded. Most of Austen's heroines are lucky enough not to fall prey to any extremes of cruelty, though Fanny Price's life at Mansfield Park, for all its tremendous privileges, will place her at the sharp end of Mrs Norris's seemingly limitless capacity for unkindness. As she fetches and carries for her aunt, Fanny experiences some of the defining features of cruelty in Austen: it makes other people useful, it derives a certain heartless pleasure from their usefulness – and it loses interest in them when that usefulness has run its course. Catherine Morland becomes persona non grata at Northanger Abbey when General Tilney is informed that she will not be a lucrative addition to his family. Willoughby coldly abandons the women whom he has seduced. Moral amnesia is a quality shared by Austen's most deplorably cruel characters.

Unkindness is everywhere in Austen but her fiction does not contain many obvious monsters. Often cruelty presents itself camouflaged as charm (Willoughby, Wickham, Walter Elliot) – or, at the very least, as accommodatingness (General Tilney). Her novels are persistently troubled by the perception that the habits of civility – polite speech, good manners, gallant gestures – can be artfully mimicked by those who have no commitment to the values that underpin them, no genuine ethical concern for the well-being of the other person. In *Sense and Sensibility*, Austen can muster at least some sympathy for Marianne Dashwood's high-minded reluctance to tell diplomatic lies in polite company (*SS*: 141). The ingratiating gestures of well-bred behaviour can function as a vehicle of unkindness rather than an antidote to it.

Although Austen's fiction contains some stand-out purveyors of cruelty, a capacity for unkindness is by no means restricted to a handful of specialists. We are all more than capable of wielding its power. In Austen's world there are always more ways to be unkind or non-kind than to be kind – purposeful cruelty is the most direct method, but botched generosity, oppressive magnanimity or intrusive over-familiarity will all get the job done. 'Nobody meant to be unkind' (*MP*: 15), the narrator remarks of the Bertrams, when a frightened and vulnerable Fanny Price is coolly received into their household. Unkindness doesn't have to be calculated or intentional; it stems, in this instance, from a certain incuriosity, a failure of ethical imagination. Fanny has been received into the Bertram home but little effort is made to understand her feelings, or to guess that they might be characterized as much by daunted homesickness as by elated gratitude. *Sense and Sensibility* opens with a comparable moment of unconscious unkindness. Henry Dashwood 'meant not to be unkind' (*SS*: 5) in his bequests to his surviving relatives, but his re-written will, itself less generous to our heroines than the original version, does nothing to protect them from the much more calculated unkindness of Fanny Dashwood. As is common in Austen's representation of **gifts**, unkindness likes to masquerade as generosity.

One of the drawbacks of excess sensibility is that it can make a person experience kindness as cruelty. Such is the response of Marianne Dashwood to Mrs Jennings, a purveyor of 'clamorous kindness' (*SS*: 245) whose bustling helpfulness and look-on-the-bright-side positivity in times of crisis tend only to exacerbate the distress of Austen's refined heroine. Acts of clumsily misjudged kindness – as when Mrs Jennings ministers to Marianne's heartbreak by plying her with sweetmeats, olives and wine – have their own unintentional cruelty in this novel. Her 'kindness is not sympathy', Marianne protests, 'her good nature is not tenderness' (*SS*: 228). If Mrs Jennings is a case study in kindness without sensibility, Marianne exhibits sensibility without kindness. Marianne will come to regret her dismissive behaviour towards Mrs Jennings as itself deficient in kindness, though even her warm tribute to 'The kindness, the unceasing kindness of Mrs Jennings' (*SS*: 392) gives a sense of how exhausting it must be for someone on the receiving end of such relentless compassion.

Writing on what he calls 'critical kindness', the philosopher William S. Hamrick makes an observation, one that is notably germane to Austen, that acts of kindness are done *for* someone and not simply *at* them or *to* them (2002: 8). Kindness *to* someone has an impersonal, one-way quality; it treats the other person as the object or even target of a compassionate intervention without addressing the specificity of that person's needs, preferences or vulnerabilities. Grandly indifferent to Fanny Price's inner life, the Bertrams in *Mansfield Park* are purveyors of an impersonal kindness *to* Austen's heroine. The honourable exception is of course Edmund Bertram, who takes time to learn about and thoughtfully attend to Fanny's unmet emotional needs. For all that Sir Thomas provides Fanny with food, shelter and education, Edmund's provision of the means for his cousin to write a **letter** to her brother seems infinitely kinder. Nor is this the only instance in Austen where a small act of kindness somehow outranks a grand one. General Tilney can effortlessly afford to host Catherine Morland at Northanger Abbey for several weeks but Eleanor Tilney's modest gift of enough money for Austen's heroine to get home safely is the more meaningfully generous gesture.

Gestures of authentic kindness in Austen often have an inconspicuous and self-contained quality. The kindness of Mr Knightley in *Emma* is deemed to be particularly admirable because it is 'un-ostentatious' (*E*: 241). Austen's work implicitly pays tribute to what Wordsworth famously describes in 'Tintern Abbey' as 'That best portion of a good man's life,/His little, nameless, unremembered, acts/Of kindness and of love'. The history of kindness, in other words, is discreetly self-erasing. Kindness does not seek publicity or reward. Even to commemorate 'acts of kindness' in a poem would potentially be a betrayal of the very self-effacingness that is part of what makes them so valuable in the first place. Just as cruelty conveniently forgets about its victims so compassion seeks no public record of its altruistic gestures. Like Wordsworth, Austen wants to honour kindness on its own self-effacing terms.

Kindness in Austen is marked by a self-effacing ability to imagine yourself in the other person's position, but the relationship between kindness and imagination in her work is by no means always a healthy one. Spuriously imagined kindness – that is, behaviour that thinks of itself as kindness or is received as kindness – is strikingly prevalent in her fiction. Lady Bertram, for example, is mightily 'struck with her own kindness' (*MP*: 322) when she offers to send Fanny her personal maid to assist in her preparations for the ball. No less self-congratulatory is Emma Woodhouse, who prides herself on 'all her kind designs' (*E*: 25) for Harriet Smith's social advancement and romantic prospects. It is no mystery why a self-regarding person such as Lady Bertram or Emma Woodhouse might entertain a flattering estimation of their own kindness. More intriguing are the reactions of those who are abjectly grateful for the kindness they believe they have received from others. Miss Bates in *Emma* is prone to see evidence of kindness everywhere and to construe herself as a wonderfully lucky recipient of neighbourly benevolence: '[H]ow kind you are!' (*E*: 412); 'So very kind! […] you are always kind' (*E*: 413); 'you are all kindness' (*E*: 496). Miss Bates is desperately eager not simply to acknowledge the kindness of her affluent **friends** and neighbours but to marvel in a public way at its extent, constancy and prevalence. One character who rivals Miss Bates in terms of abject thankfulness for imagined kindness is Mr Collins in *Pride and Prejudice*. Collins is consumed by servile thankfulness for the 'kindness' of Lady Catherine de Bourgh (*PP*: 240), a patron whose glacial unfriendliness and imperious bossiness he somehow manages to construe as evidence of warm and wholehearted moral support. Collins and Miss Bates don't have much in common, but there is a strong element of narcissism in their ecstasies of gratitude – a thrilled sense that it's *me* who has been singled out for kind attention.

Austen's writings are frequently troubled by the perception that we routinely overinvest in kindness because it is what we have instead of justice and equality in an unfair society. Miss Bates and Mr Collins have a peculiar talent for seeing kindness when it isn't there. They re-write hierarchical relationships of power as heart-warming stories of compassion, and they greet their own subordinate positions in those power-structures as evidence of spectacular good fortune. In a world where the likes of Lady Catherine revel imperiously in their own privilege while decent, vulnerable people slide irreversibly into poverty, the language of kindness spreads reassuring fantasies about interpersonal goodwill that transcends and disguises social divisions. Everyone is shocked – including, retrospectively, Emma herself – when Austen's heroine is 'so brutal, so cruel to Miss Bates!' (*E*: 409) on Box Hill. But perhaps her decision to humiliate Miss Bates stands out not as an unpardonable lapse in kindness but rather as a rare moment of honesty in a world where Miss Bates's humiliating poverty – indeed the hardships and humiliations of poverty itself – is accepted as an unarguable fact of nature. The effects of a system that is 'so brutal, so cruel' to the **poor** are not significantly alleviated by the language of kindness. Austen does not articulate these insights in explicitly political terms but they are readable, all the same, in her searching explorations of kindness and its limitations. There is never enough kindness in the world – and kindness is never enough.

L IS FOR LETTER

Letters are woven into the fabric of Austen's life and literary career. Immersed in the humdrum minutiae of her existence – shopping, weather, neighbours – the letters to her sister Cassandra bring us as close as we're ever going to get to the texture of everyday life as they experienced it. The hundreds of letters that Cassandra destroyed a couple of years before her death, meanwhile, will always be the most excruciatingly tantalizing gap in our knowledge of the author's personal life. The letter, both as narrative form and as cultural object, is also a crucial component of Austen's fiction. Her most ambitious teenage works, from 'Love and Freindship' to *Lady Susan*, are written in an epistolary mode that takes inspiration from major predecessors such as Frances Burney and Samuel Richardson. On the face of it, Austen renounces this mode in her mature work; her full-length novels, with their anonymous narrators and coolly detached irony, seem to distance her art from the unfiltered outpourings of feeling associated with the letters of eighteenth-century sentimental fiction (see Watson 1994: 87–108). However, an 'underlying epistolary scaffolding' (Davidson 2017: 14) continues to be visible to the naked **eye** in Austen long after she officially abandons the form. The informational ecosystems of mature works from *Northanger Abbey* to *Sanditon* simply wouldn't function without the letters in which Austen's characters share news, express emotion, consolidate and sustain friendships and relationships, close geographical gaps, deliver advice, ask for money, express gratitude, calibrate intimacy and re-negotiate distance.

Austen is always interested in letters' existence and circulation as objects – who holds them, how they get paid for, transported, delivered, handed round, stored, destroyed or even, as in the case of a crucial note from Frank Churchill to **Jane** Fairfax (*E*: 482), absent-mindedly locked away. Whether it's a cri de coeur or a perfunctory memo, a letter is a material artefact whose production and transmission costs time and resources. To save paper, Austen would often cram every inch of her letters with writing, sometimes turning them upside-down to squeeze extra material between the gaps, and sometimes turning them at right angles in order to 'cross-write' further text across what had already been written (see Van Ostade 2014: 6–7). Austen's heroines often share her appreciation of the letter as both an everyday necessity and a precious luxury. In *Mansfield Park*, Edmund enables the isolated and homesick Fanny to write home to Portsmouth by providing pen, ink and paper, and by assuring her that Sir Thomas will 'frank' the letter – that is, he will use his parliamentary privileges to send the letter free of charge.

'Frank' is a word whose various meanings echo quietly but persistently through what turns out to be Austen's most letter-obsessed novel. A text about the surreptitious letter-writing habits of a man called Frank, *Emma* is, as Valentine Cunningham puts it, the story of 'the unfrank doings of the unfrank franker of unfrank letters Frank Churchill' (1994: 337). Frank Churchill is by no means the leading protagonist of this novel but between them Frank and his secret fiancée Jane Fairfax, whose relationship is conducted almost exclusively in letters, represent an alternative centre of gravity for *Emma*, one in which all the most compelling narratives are routed through the postal system. *Emma* represents a high point of Austen's achievement in the art of subtly modulated third-person narrative, but Frank and Jane might be said to 'cross-write' this text by making themselves the protagonists of their own clandestine epistolary novel.

The postal system that grants Jane Fairfax a private life also grants Jane Austen access to the private mental worlds of her characters. Letters serve to vary and complicate the texture of her narratives; they allow the perspective to switch, in a brief and self-contained way, from third- to first-person, plunging us into a particular character's version of reality, their private linguistic world. When Lydia Bennet writes to brief Harriet Forster about her elopement with Wickham, her letter strikes a note of giddy exhilaration ('You will laugh when you know where I am gone [...] I cannot help laughing myself [...] I can hardly write for laughing' [*PP*: 321]) that is startlingly at odds with the sombre mood back at Longbourn. Lydia's excitable note to Mrs Forster is just one entry in a frantic flurry of correspondence that breaks out around her elopement. Jane Bennet anxiously breaks the news to Elizabeth (*PP*: 301–4); Mr Collins moralizes insufferably about Lydia's 'heinous offence' (*PP*: 327–8); Mr Gardiner offers reassurance and practical support (*PP*: 325–6, 333–4, 345–6). In early works such as 'Lesley Castle', where Margaret Lesley and Lady Lesley impart conflicting versions of one another to a shared epistolary confidante, Austen had explored the comic possibilities that are opened up when letter-writers offer different versions of and verdicts on the same circumstances. At this crucial moment in *Pride and Prejudice*, when letters become tools of reputation-management and damage-limitation, she uses the epistolary mode to dramatize uncertainty in the context of an unfolding crisis. The complex psychological truth of a given situation in Austen often emerges only in the contrast between rival eye-witness accounts transmitted through letters. In *Mansfield Park*, Fanny Price obtains a new and illuminating vantage-point on events in Northamptonshire when she is away from the place and in receipt of conflicting updates from the Bertrams. Lady Bertram's complacently upbeat reports on Tom's health, for example, clash notably with Edmund's far less reassuring assessment of his brother's perilous condition. Although Austen has officially turned her back on epistolarity, the dramatic substance of her novels continues to be glimpsed, filtered and contested in significant ways through letters.

Flick through the pages of an Austen novel and you will tend to see more letters in the second half. The shift to a more epistolary mode is especially evident in *Northanger Abbey* and *Mansfield Park*, where exchanges of letters mark the distance between a group of **friends** and family previously centred in one key locale who have now been dispersed by events. Letters in these novels are at one and the same time a vital lifeline between scattered friends and family and the symptom of a crisis of separation and estrangement. Seemingly intimate friendships are re-negotiated and often cancelled in these interludes of intense correspondence. The falseness of false friends is never disclosed more transparently than in the letters they write to Austen's heroines. Even a cursory glance at the correspondence of Isabella Thorpe to Catherine Morland in *Northanger Abbey* or Lucy Steele to Elinor Dashwood in *Sense and Sensibility* should be enough to dispel any uncertainty about our verdict on these eminently unreliable characters. Not quite so easy to dismiss are the two longest letters in Austen's fiction, both of which are the work of a man who wants to write himself back into respectability after behaving in inexplicable, underhand or hurtful ways. In *Pride and Prejudice*, Darcy writes at length to set the record straight after his acrimonious rejection by Elizabeth (*PP*: 218–25) while in *Emma* Frank Churchill writes to his stepmother, Mrs Weston, to beg forgiveness for his wayward and secretive behaviour (*E*: 476–83). In both cases, a male letter-writer claims a formidable amount of textual space – but their female readers have the privilege of accepting or rejecting these lengthy male-authored accounts of recent history.

Austen's heroines are not great letter-writers, but they are frequently seen as recipients and readers of letters. Often her heroines occupy a position of expectant helplessness as they wait for letters that may never come – or that may bring them news of a world that is beyond their reach and out of their control. The letter can be viewed, by its recipient, as both an object of desire and a source of fear. Catherine Morland, when she arrives at Northanger Abbey, waits 'nine successive mornings' (*NA*: 207) on a letter from Isabella Thorpe. When she arrives in London, Marianne Dashwood waits with mounting desperation for any word from Willoughby. Fanny Price, for whom the postman's knock is a source of 'daily terrors' (*MP*: 462), is said to 'live upon letters' (*MP*: 496) when she returns from Northamptonshire to Portsmouth.

If waiting for letters consigns Austen's heroines to a position of isolated, fretful passivity, reading letters can be an altogether more active and sociable business. In *Persuasion*, when Mrs Smith shows Anne Elliot a letter from William Elliot to Charles Smith denouncing Sir Walter in strongly disrespectful terms, Austen's heroine is uncomfortably aware that 'no private correspondence could bear the eye of others' (*P*: 221). It's just as well that few characters in Austen are inhibited by ethical scruples from reading letters that weren't addressed to them. Correspondence in her social worlds frequently finds an audience beyond its official addressee and indeed comes to life in the eyes of a community of readers. Frank Churchill's letters to his aunt make him a minor celebrity in Highbury. Catherine Morland, when she returns home to Fullerton, maintains a 'clandestine correspondence' (*NA*: 259) with Eleanor Tilney, knowing that her brother Henry may be a secondary audience for her letters. In *Emma*, Robert Martin's letter of proposal to Harriet Smith finds a secondary audience in the person of Emma, who is disconcerted by the letter's 'bewitching flattery' (*E*: 55). Letters in Austen can also have more than one writer. When Emma reads Robert Martin's proposal to Harriet, she suspects that he may have had the help of one of his sisters in drafting it (*E*: 53); she, in turn, will do more than help draft Harriet's letter of rejection. In *Sense and Sensibility*, the letter in which Willoughby effectively disavows his relationship with Marianne is dictated by the woman to whom he is engaged, the heiress Miss Grey (*SS*: 372) – a rare moment of cross-gender ghost-writing in Austen. In *Mansfield Park*, Henry Crawford becomes an unofficial co-author of his sister's correspondence, flirtatiously annotating Mary's letters to Fanny Price. Framed as a private narrative directed from one named individual to another, the personal letter in Austen is a complex social artefact, a space where multiple authors and multiple readers encounter one another.

Letter-reading is a significant social activity in Austen, one that frequently reveals as much about those reading as it does about the text under consideration. A case in point is Mr Collins's wonderfully pompous letter of introduction to Mr Bennet, a text so rich in self-regard that Elizabeth's father can't resist reading it aloud to his family (*PP*: 69–70). The letter provokes a remarkably varied range of reactions in the Bennet household. Jane is open-minded and characteristically generous. Elizabeth is quizzically critical of Collins's pompous style. Mr Bennet openly relishes the letter's absurd self-importance. Mary delivers a wooden appreciation of its rhetoric. Mrs Bennet, previously ill-disposed towards Collins, seems to have been won over by his grandly conciliatory words. Lydia and Kitty, meanwhile, are united by their indifference to what they've heard. The letter tells us all we need to know about Collins – nothing in his subsequent behaviour will contradict the portrait of insufferable self-regard that it paints – but its reception at Longbourn also provides a most revealing group portrait of the Bennet family.

Letters in Austen reach multiple readers and may also, in turn, provoke multiple readings and interpretations. They are pored over, quoted with admiration, incredulity or scorn, sifted for revealing details, scanned for subtext. Shared and recited, they provide the basis of harmless 'parlor entertainment' (Wheeler 1998: 37) but also stir up anticipation, anxiety and uncertainty. When Bingley seems to have vanished from Jane's life, Elizabeth dedicates herself to re-reading all of her sister's letters, scouring them for evidence of unhappiness (*PP*: 210). Darcy's long letter to Elizabeth in the aftermath of his first, unsuccessful proposal is one that she will 'read, and re-read with the closest attention' (*PP*: 227) to the point of knowing it off by heart. Later still she reads Mrs Gardiner's commendation of Darcy 'again and again' (*PP*: 361) with trembling hopefulness. 'What do you think of *this* sentence, my dear Lizzy?' (*PP*: 132), asks Jane, as they pore over a letter from Caroline Bingley announcing her family's removal from Netherfield to London. Reading and re-reading letters together creates and sustains intimacy even when the letter in question is vexingly laconic. Austen's heroines often have to subsist on a meagre diet of news, so it's no surprise that they will seize on whatever scraps of narrative a letter might contain. The informational substance and emotional nuances of a letter can never be exhausted in one sitting. The letter is an ephemeral genre but Austen's re-readers make it their business to eke out enough precious meaning from their correspondence to sustain them until the postman's next **visit**. Implicitly dramatized in Austen's representation of compulsive letter reading and re-reading is her own powerful and long-standing attachment to the epistolary genre. Long after she seems to renounce the epistolary form, her fiction continues to 'live upon letters'.

M IS FOR MATCHMAKING

When Austen gathered together some of the earliest verdicts on *Emma*, one of its less enthusiastic readers was her old **friend** and neighbour Alethea Bigg, who reportedly 'objected to the sameness of the subject (Match-making) all through' ('Opinions of *Emma*', *LM*: 235–6). Bigg was by no means wrong to say that matchmaking is a persistent topic of concern in *Emma*, as indeed it is in many of Austen's writings. Every Austen novel is a courtship story, and every Austen novel contains those who are impatiently eager for courtship to be fast-tracked. From Mrs Bennet in *Pride and Prejudice* to Mrs Jennings in *Sense and Sensibility* to Emma Woodhouse in *Emma*, Austen's matchmakers are not content simply to be cheerleaders for matrimony – they want to make vigorously pro-active efforts to convert unattached individuals into married couples.

What's in it for them? It's fair to say that Austen's matchmakers are motivated by more than disinterested concern for the happiness and well-being of others. Economic self-interest and social prestige are often key factors. If Mrs Bennet's daughters marry well, her whole family wins. If Darcy marries Anne de Bourgh then Lady Catherine de Bourgh will have played her part in consolidating a prestigious alliance between two ancient families. A fondness for matchmaking can also be a symptom of privileged boredom. With her two daughters respectably married, Mrs Jennings has 'nothing to do but to marry all the rest of the world' (*SS*: 43). Emma Woodhouse, for whom matchmaking is the 'greatest amusement in the world!' (*E*: 10), also has a hobbyistic relation with the private lives of others, not to mention a competitive desire to be the first with any breaking news about romantic relationships in the neighbourhood.

No one in Austen ever asks to be match-made. Although de facto systems of matchmaking seem to be more or less permanently at work in her social worlds, her heroines are never happy for romantic decisions and preferences to be outsourced to a third party. What is more, the successfully partnered characters in her fiction would be able to tell you that the positive outcomes of their courtship narratives owe little to the efforts of matchmakers.

Interventionist champions of romantic love in Austen can be wilfully oblivious to the sensibilities and scruples of those whom they try to match, often mistaking caution for self-defeating timidity or proper discretion for self-advertising coyness. They tend blithely to overestimate the accuracy of their own judgements about the suitability and compatibility of others, and to overstate the role they play in bringing couples together. A particular speciality of Austen's matchmakers is a kind of self-congratulatory magical thinking that claims credit for what would have happened anyway. Emma Woodhouse is delighted at the role she believes she has played in uniting Miss Taylor with Mr Weston, but who's to say she is any less deluded than Mrs Bennet is when she takes credit for the rain shower that detains **Jane** at Netherfield (*PP*: 34)?

Austen's matchmakers are also oblivious to the potentially disruptive and harmful effects of their interventions. Eager efforts to bring people together – such as Mrs Bennet's painfully obvious attempts to match Jane Bennet with Charles Bingley – **risk** unintentionally sabotaging the very relationships that they are trying to bring about. Indeed, it seems at times as though a law of unintended consequences operates in relation to endeavours in the field of matchmaking. Successful relationships frequently owe their existence not to the benign efforts of matchmakers but to the obstructive interference of saboteurs. General Tilney blocks a potential match between Henry Tilney and Catherine Morland, Emma Woodhouse endeavours to separate Harriet Smith from Robert Martin, Sir Walter Elliot and Lady Russell dissuade Anne Elliot from marrying Wentworth – but in all of these cases officious interference only gives the relationship a chance to prove itself over time. The obstructive and destructive figure of the match-breaker might seem to be the archenemy of the matchmaker in Austen's world, but in practice her match-breakers have a surprisingly successful track record of bringing people together.

Are there *any* good matchmakers in Austen? A rare example of genuinely effective practice in the field is modelled by Mr and Mrs Gardiner in *Pride and Prejudice*, the relatives with whom Elizabeth travels to Derbyshire and in whose company she is reunited with Mr Darcy at his most conspicuously eligible. Once they cotton on to the obvious attraction between Elizabeth and Darcy, the Gardiners are enthusiastic about the match but not in a way that intrudes too insensitively on the private emotional lives of this potential couple. Their most pointedly interventionist gesture is a comment in a **letter** from Mrs Gardiner to Elizabeth to the effect that Darcy 'wants nothing but a little more liveliness, and *that*, if he marry *prudently*, his wife may teach him' (*PP*: 360). With its focus on the way a man's needs will be met by the wife he does not yet have, this comment echoes the matchmaking language of the novel's opening sentence. Mrs Gardiner, in other words, has joined the ranks of the matchmakers whose voices the novel has ventriloquized from the outset. Miraculously, however, the Gardiners manage to do their bit for Elizabeth's romantic prospects without embarrassing her. Here, the key seems to be the difference between a matchmaker who clumsily tries to force a couple into existence and a non-interventionist or laissez-faire one who provides a benign context for a relationship to happen, as far as possible, on its own terms. The ambition of such a matchmaker is to make the marriage between the two parties in question seem like the obvious, default choice – not so much a choice, indeed, as an inevitable outcome that is waiting for them at the end of an effortless journey down the path of least resistance.

When Austen satirizes matchmaking it is often because of its tactless indifference to the feelings and preferences of the potential couple in question. Matchmaking, as practised by, say, Mrs Bennet is a small but persistent crime against decorum and sensibility. But there are ways in which matchmaking is loyal – and, indeed, embarrassingly open in its loyalty – to some of the unspoken norms of Austen's social worlds. In their efforts to 'marry all the rest of the world', matchmakers throw their weight behind what modern readers influenced by **queer** theory would recognize as 'compulsory heterosexuality' – the notion that it is the natural destiny and social duty of any unattached person to establish a lifelong relationship with a romantic partner of the opposite sex. This ideology is never glimpsed more clearly than in the opening words of *Pride and Prejudice*, with their matchmaker's-eye view of social reality. The culture of compulsory heterosexuality is one for which matchmakers volunteer as a kind of neighbourhood enforcement patrol whose job it is to round up unattached people and get them married off. But here we run into a paradox. On the one hand, heterosexual romance is deemed to be as natural and inevitable as the turning of the seasons; on the other, couples don't form themselves spontaneously and at times must be artfully chivvied into existence. Matchmakers subscribe to the ideology of compulsory heterosexuality, but not so strongly as to trust that the ideology will succeed without assistance. The system could always do with a bit of help. What makes matchmaking embarrassing, then, is not simply that it causes **young** people to squirm at the antics of a Mrs Bennet or a Mrs Jennings. More than this, the very existence of matchmaking as a cultural practice is embarrassing for a system that wouldn't need matchmakers if it was as seamlessly natural as it purports to be.

The figure of the matchmaker – embarrassing, blundering, ineffective – is, nevertheless, a useful person to have in the pages of an Austen novel. A number of critics (Tanner 2007: 199; Raff 2014: 9–10) have remarked on the analogy between matchmaking and storytelling, and it's easy to see the matchmaker as a kind of second-rate *alter ego* for the novelist – one whose efforts to take control of the narrative, to shape and direct its love stories, are divertingly and reassuringly incompetent. Consider, for example, the misadventures and misreadings of the various matchmakers in *Emma*. The heroine tries to engineer a match between Harriet Smith and Mr Elton, she imagines a secret attachment between Jane Fairfax and Mr Dixon, and later begins to wonder about a match between Frank Churchill and Harriet Smith. Mr Weston hopes Frank will pair off with Emma while Mrs Weston imagines a romantic future for Mr Knightley and Jane Fairfax. The residents of Highbury can't not see couples everywhere, and this kind of compulsive 'double vision' is comic in its persistent faultiness. The local gossips are right to suspect the existence of possible romantic pairings everywhere – this is, after all, a Jane Austen novel – but their specific predictions and prophecies about these couples-in-the-making are consistently wide of the mark. In this novel of enthusiastic but fallible pundits, every blunder perpetrated by the heroine and her fellow Highbury matchmakers serves to reinforce Austen's implied authority over the outcomes of its romantic storylines.

Austen's fiction has a permanently conflicted relationship with matchmakers and matchmaking. On the one hand, it wants to expose their hobby to a series of pointed satirical objections; on the other, it wants to outperform them at that same hobby. Austen presents her courtship narratives as grand matchmaking schemes that succeed where Mrs Jennings, Mrs Bennet, Emma et al so conspicuously fail; indeed, they seem to succeed precisely *because* her matchmakers make such a dependable hash of things. Even so, Austen can't quite decide whether her matchmakers are really bad at matchmaking – or whether matchmaking, however scrupulously practised, is itself something bad, unnecessary and objectionable. She can't attack matchmaking without at the same time attacking the grammar of her own fiction. Even as she derides matchmakers she can't help catching, in the mirror of their behaviour, unflattering glimpses of the matrimonial obsessions that drive her own novels. And Austen gives us other reasons to reflect self-critically on the kind of satirical fun that her fiction has at the expense of matchmakers. Imagine being obsessed by other people's marriage prospects. Imagine living vicariously through the romantic adventures of family, friends and neighbours. Imagine talking volubly and constantly about the love lives of single people. Imagine making your pleasure contingent on the outcomes of their romantic choices. Austen's readers, as they ponder the amusing flaws of her matchmakers, might experience a mild shock of recognition. Her fiction, as Martin Amis has remarked, 'makes Mrs Bennets of us all' (2001: 433).

N IS FOR NO

On 2 December 1802, Austen received – and accepted – a proposal of marriage from a family **friend**, Harris Bigg-Wither, the 21-year-old son of one of her old neighbours in Hampshire. She had second thoughts, and retracted her consent the next morning. The author's niece, Caroline Lloyd, would later report that she had always respected her aunt for 'cancelling that yes' (cited in Le Faye 2004: 138). In rejecting Bigg-Wither, Austen had recourse to one of the few distinctive powers available to women in a male-dominated society: what Henry Tilney, in *Northanger Abbey*, calls the 'power of refusal' (*NA*: 74). 'The power of refusal', as modelled by Tilney, is not exactly a superpower. By its nature limited and negative, it is the power to reject possible scenarios, interactions or relationships rather than to propose or initiate them. In Austen's world there is a taboo around women articulating their desires, but at certain crucial junctures they can say, emphatically, what they don't want. This power is wielded many times, and in many different ways, by her heroines, who continually find themselves having to reject romantic overtures, deliver knockbacks to would-be suitors, opt out of unappealing social initiatives and stand their ground against peer pressure. In *Northanger Abbey*, Catherine Morland refuses to accompany her brother and the Thorpes on an excursion to Clifton. In *Mansfield Park*, Fanny declines the opportunity to join the cast of *Lovers' Vows*. In *The Watsons*, Emma Watson declines Tom Musgrave's invitation to **dance**, rejects his offer of a ride home in his curricle – and it will surely be only a matter of time before she is rebuffing an offer of marriage from the same source. One of the distinctive challenges for anyone coming out into the world is learning to reject a lot of what it has to offer. To be an Austen heroine is to spend an awful lot of time saying *no*. Indeed, you could say that her heroines only really to come into their own as autonomous characters when they begin to discover and explore their powers of veto. Their emerging identities – and indeed the overall shape of Austen's storylines – are to a remarkable extent structured by refusals.

Saying no, in a culture of elegant people-pleasing, is never easy. Austen makes a joke of this in her early tale 'Frederic and Elfrida' when Charlotte accepts marriage proposals from two different men on the same day because she hates disappointing people. 'No' is arguably the most powerful item in an Austen heroine's vocabulary, but the word's powers do not necessarily belong to the person who utters it. 'It will be safer to say "No," perhaps', says Harriet Smith in *Emma*, as she ponders a proposal of marriage from the respectable farmer Robert Martin. 'Do you think I had better say "No?"' (*E*: 55). 'No' is a word that Emma's friend virtually picks up with tweezers, conscious as she is that its potential effects – to inflict grave disappointment and to close down opportunities that may not present themselves in the future – are ones that lie beyond her control.

As she weighs the **risks** and benefits of saying no to Martin, Harriet occupies a position that most Austen heroines will at some stage find themselves in. Elizabeth Bennet rejects Mr Collins and (first time round) Darcy; Fanny Price rejects Henry Crawford; Emma Woodhouse rejects Mr Elton; and Anne Elliot rejects Wentworth (first time round) and Charles Musgrove. The moment of acceptance, and its immediate aftermath, is rarely dramatized by Austen in any detailed or sustained way. She tends not to stick around when proposals are successful, as though she wants to grant the happy couples their privacy – and also to acknowledge that her narratives have run their course when the heroine says yes. Rejection scenes are different. If all successful proposals in Austen are the same, every rejected one fails in its own distinctive way. Her refusal scenes are, accordingly, staged with considerable vividness and variety, sometimes exploiting the abundant comic possibilities of the situation, sometimes focusing on the distress and vexation occasioned by an unwanted suitor who won't take no for an answer.

A curious marginal case of refusal occurs in *Northanger Abbey*, where John Thorpe broaches the subject of marriage to Catherine Morland in such an ineptly roundabout way that she does not even take the hint that he is making a significant declaration of romantic interest. Austen's heroine doesn't say 'no' here because she does not construe Thorpe's words as a coded proposal; she doesn't have to reject Thorpe because his implicit proposal of marriage simply doesn't make itself heard. In time, when Isabella Thorpe provides a more candid account of her brother's romantic intentions, Catherine will say that: 'I certainly cannot return his affection' (*NA*: 148). As is common in Austen, the language of rejection here is couched in terms of *ability* – in terms of what the heroine can and can't do – rather than preference or discretion. Proposals, even when they are emphatically unwelcome, are usually declined in a tone of meek, respectful and conciliatory self-deprecation. The heroine cannot return the suitor's affection, much as it pains her to say so, and she passes no explicit judgement on the personal qualities of the proposer when she delivers the bad news. Fanny Price explains to Sir Thomas Bertram that she has rejected Henry Crawford because it is 'quite out of my power to return his good opinion' (*MP*: 363) while Elizabeth Bennet, when fending off the romantic overtures of Mr Collins, explains that 'it is impossible for me to do otherwise than decline' (*PP*: 120). The refusal scene is a rare moment when women get to tell patriarchy what it doesn't want to hear, but the refuser is usually careful not to overplay her hand. The moment of refusal is a powerful gesture disguised as an apologetic declaration of incapacity.

The impact of the refusal scene, and its personal toll on the refuser, hinges on the balance of power between the refuser and refusee. Emma Woodhouse can swat Mr Elton away in the knowledge that she risks nothing by doing so; Fanny Price's rejection of Henry Crawford, on the other hand, is from a position of comparative vulnerability and precarity. The power behind a heroine's refusal can be measured in terms of the extent to which it succeeds in closing down an unwanted conversation. When Collins is rejected by Elizabeth Bennet he blithely asserts that 'it is usual with **young** ladies to reject the addresses of the man whom they secretly mean to accept' (*PP*: 120). It so happens that Elizabeth will indeed have a change of heart about another suitor, Darcy, whom she had previously rejected. But this doesn't make Collins any less obnoxious or obtuse in his determination to hear her 'no' only as a coy or delayed 'yes'. Nor is Collins the only man in Austen who refuses to be refused. When Knightley expresses disbelief and frustration at Harriet's refusal of Robert Martin, Emma replies with exasperated sarcasm: 'Oh! to be sure […] it is always incomprehensible to a man that a woman should ever refuse an offer of marriage' (*E*: 64). Such strategic incomprehension is deployed with special tenacity by Henry Crawford in *Mansfield Park*. When the heroine declines his offer of marriage, the relationship between them develops into an asymmetrical battle of refusals in which he refuses to hear her 'No, no, no' (*MP*: 349) as anything but a potential yes. Fanny's 'No, no, no' will have to prolong itself over many chapters.

Whenever a potential suitor is refused, Austen's fiction gives us at least some scope to imagine an alternative timeline in which the heroine might have said yes. It is hinted more than once in *Mansfield Park* that Fanny might have accepted Crawford (*MP*: 518, 526–7, 540). *Persuasion* asks us to imagine how things might have turned out if Anne Elliot had accepted Wentworth first time round. Some of these alternative futures are more imaginable than others. You could have a bit of counterfactual fun imagining what married life would have been like if Elizabeth Bennet had agreed to become Mrs Collins, but the clergyman's proposal was never going to be successful. Part of his spectacular failure is that the possibility of rejection has never even crossed his mind. His proposal does not frame itself as a request that may or may not be granted but rather as a statement, unintentionally comical in its elaborate formality, of the reasoning behind his decision to get married. Collins does not speak to Elizabeth as to someone who has her own, as yet undeclared, feelings and opinions about her romantic status; rather, he speaks of a time 'when we are married' (*PP*: 120) as a fait accompli. His suit to her is a masterclass in how not to propose.

As a rule, the chances of a proposal being successful in Austen are in inverse proportion to the confidence with which it is delivered. '[T]he right proposal', as Mullan points out, 'is the one that can imagine the answer "no"' (2012: 287). Consider, by contrast to Collins, the fearful uncertainty with which Knightley proposes to Emma Woodhouse: 'Say "No," if it is to be said' (*E*: 468). Part of his proposal's persuasive authenticity lies in the way it has already incorporated the concept of refusal – that tiny, devastating word *no* – into its own phrasing.

The refusal scene, in Austen, seems to position women at a point of maximum strength and men at a point of maximum vulnerability. The word 'no' is a potentially devastating linguistic weapon but its power don't always come from the refuser. Sometimes – as when the young Anne Elliot breaks off her engagement with Wentworth – the 'no' comes from her family and friends. When it meets with resistance, the female 'no' may need to borrow power and authority from a male voice in order to make itself heard. When Elizabeth Bennet can't prevail upon Mr Collins to accept her negative answer, her final recourse is to her father, whose 'negative […] must be decisive' (*PP*: 122). When the power of the heroine's 'no' is underwritten by her father, then the refusal scene, the great set-piece of female autonomy in a patriarchal world, turns out to be another male-dominated conversation.

In Austen's refusal scenes, what should be a decisive moment of clarification often becomes painfully muddied and prolonged. Despite this, it's fair to say that the Austen heroine is never wrong in her refusals, even when – like Elizabeth Bennet or Anne Elliot – she later changes her mind. The exception to this rule is Emma Woodhouse. There is no question that the heroine of *Emma* is right to rebuff Mr Elton's proposal of marriage. Her (admittedly somewhat narcissistic) fantasy of rejecting a proposal from

N is for No

Frank Churchill (*E*: 284) also seems to represent a sensible verdict on their likely compatibility. What the novel cannot bring itself to endorse, however, is the general rule that Emma infers from these specific refusals – the fantasy that, in refusing this or that suitor, she is refusing matrimony itself. Alone among Austen's heroines, Emma's ambition is 'never to marry' (*E*: 284). It's probably fair to guess that no one with a more than passing familiarity with Austen's work will read this novel under the impression that the heroine is going to stick to her 'resolution of never marrying' (*E*: 128). Whether or not we notice that Mr Knightley is hidden in plain sight from the very first chapter as Emma's husband-to-be, the novel amounts to a 500-page rebuttal of its heroine's fantasy of life without marriage. Emma can explicitly refuse Mr Elton and implicitly refuse Frank Churchill, but her refusal of marriage is itself refused by the novel. Emma says 'no' to marriage but the novel emphatically cancels that no. A Jane Austen heroine can't not get married. Emma Woodhouse wields the power of refusal with exceptional self-assurance, but the matrimonial destiny that the novel arranges for its heroine is in the end an offer she can't refuse.

O IS FOR OBSTACLE

Elizabeth Bennet and Mr Darcy first encounter one another in chapter three of *Pride and Prejudice*, but nearly sixty further chapters will elapse before they finally declare their love for one another and get married. What takes them so long? In the same novel Charlotte Lucas and Mr Collins, who get married within eight chapters of meeting one another, show that it can all be done in a fraction of the time. However, whereas Charlotte's journey to the altar is impressively – indeed startlingly – seamless, Elizabeth and Darcy have to negotiate a veritable obstacle course of psychological and cultural barriers before they can arrive at their happy ending. These obstacles are attitudinal (she is prejudiced, he is proud – and, to some extent, *vice versa*); socio-economic (Darcy is considerably richer, and moves in much more prestigious social circles, than Elizabeth); familial (with the exception of **Jane**, most of Elizabeth's family contrive to embarrass her in Darcy's **eyes**); geographical (Darcy is, quite simply, elsewhere and out of reach for much of the novel); and epistemological (their relationship is plagued by misunderstandings from the outset). Sometimes, obstacles can manifest themselves in the guise of one exceptionally obstructive person. Darcy's formidable aunt, Lady Catherine De Bourgh, has her own plans for her nephew and vehemently opposes the match with Elizabeth. Wickham – a rival candidate for Elizabeth's affections who spreads defamatory misinformation about Darcy and becomes a source of family embarrassment for the Bennets – is an even more problematic impediment between the two. As we begin to itemize the various barriers that lie between Elizabeth and Darcy, it seems a miracle that they get married at all. And that's before we even mention the biggest obstacle of all, a kind of super-obstacle that trumps any of those listed here – the obstacle of the novel itself. If Elizabeth and Darcy *had* got married in chapter four of *Pride and Prejudice* then the novel as we know and love it wouldn't have happened. The marriage can't happen because of the all the obstacles that lie in its way, but the novel can't happen without those very obstacles. *Pride and Prejudice* is the story of everything that gets in the way of the story.

Any Austen novel can be read as a constantly updated map of the relative positions of the hero and the heroine and the obstacles that lie between them. In *Persuasion*, when Wentworth is on active service in the **West Indies**, Anne Elliot is separated from him by the expanse of the Atlantic Ocean. The gap between them will shrink to half a mile when he re-locates, unexpectedly and thrillingly, to Somerset. Soon there will be nothing between them but the width of a hedgerow (*P*: 93) or a single person's body on the sofa (*P*: 73). To be sure, a formidable set of intangible barriers continues to lie between Anne and Wentworth, but the steadily dwindling physical distance between the two points always to the possibility of a blissfully unobstructed reunion between the estranged lovers.

Sometimes clearing obstacles can seem like the easiest thing in the world. Nothing captures Elizabeth Bennet's energy, wilfulness and spirited good nature more vividly than the sight of her 'jumping over stiles and springing over puddles' (*PP*: 36) as she makes her way from Longbourn to Netherfield, there to tend to her beloved sister Jane. Obstacles lie across her path but she negotiates them with pleasurable ease. A Jane Austen heroine's journey from the family home to the grand country house has never been simpler. But things will look different in retrospect. Elizabeth's carefree traipse to Netherfield is an almost suspiciously effortless warm-up for what will be an altogether more fraught and demanding trek – the strenuous, roundabout journey that she will undertake from Longbourn to married life at Pemberley.

Elizabeth's walk to Netherfield can be read as a conveniently self-contained allegorical version of a journey that all of Austen's heroines will make across a landscape of obstacles – physical, psychological and cultural – towards an object of desire. Here and elsewhere, the complex relationship between obstacles and human desire is explored by her novels in ways that invite comparison with modern psychoanalytic thought. In a discerning meditation on the 'twinning' (1994: 82) of obstacles and desire, Adam Phillips argues that the relation between the two is never less than intricately shifting and paradoxical. Obstacles stand in the way of what we want; they block our desires. But at some level we need these obstacles. It is impossible to think about desire without thinking about what might prevent us from acting on it or fulfilling it. And such blockages can inflame the very desires that they seek to prohibit. Consider, in this regard, what happens when Henry Crawford and Maria Bertram confront the locked gate at the ha-ha at Sotherton Court in *Mansfield Park*. Nowhere in Austen is there a more imposing architectural manifestation of the taboos and prohibitions that lie between her characters and their illicit desires. But the gate and the ha-ha, those formal boundaries between the civilized decorum of the country house and the great outdoors of uninhibited desire, present Henry and Maria with an irresistible opportunity for the thrill of transgression. When they slip by this barrier, while Maria's fiancé, Mr Rushworth, goes off in the search of the key, they enact a very public dress rehearsal for their adulterous liaison. Transgression becomes thinkable, in other words, when we are confronted with sharp borders and no-go areas.

Not all obstacles in Austen are as visible and obvious as the gate and the ha-ha. The most difficult obstacles to negotiate are the ones that we might not recognize as such. In *Northanger Abbey*, when Catherine Morland declares her intention to join the Tilneys for a country walk, John Thorpe does his best to keep her to himself by insisting that 'I never saw so much dirt in my life […] you could no more walk than you could fly! […] it is ancle-deep every where' (*NA*: 84). Thorpe's visions of ankle-deep mud, as Catherine will soon observe, are a pure fabrication. But the non-existent mud stands for a very real obstacle in the heroine's path – that is, the 'dirt' of Thorpe's incontinent and shameless bluster in which the truth is continually blurred, smudged and distorted. In a novel of problematic journeys, none will be more challenging for *Northanger Abbey*'s heroine than the one she makes through a social landscape that is ankle-deep in the sludge of lies and exaggerations.

What can Austen's characters do to negotiate the obstacles in their way? The answer to this question partly depends on whether we are talking about primary or secondary characters. Many of her secondary female characters – Charlotte Lucas in *Pride and Prejudice*, Isabella Thorpe in *Northanger Abbey*, Mrs Clay in *Persuasion* – display a considerable amount of hustle and pragmatism as they confront obstacles on the road to happiness. Lucy Steele, Elinor Dashwood's rival and bête noire in *Sense and Sensibility*, is exemplary in this regard. A social climber who ends up advantageously married to Robert Ferrars, Lucy is described as 'a most encouraging instance of what an earnest, an unceasing attention to self-interest, however its progress may be apparently obstructed, will do in securing every advantage of fortune, with no other sacrifice than that of time and conscience' (*SS*: 426). This tribute to Lucy's vulgar success story is, of course, witheringly ironic. Her road to happiness is paved with selfishness and opportunism. No Austen heroine would be permitted to pursue her own economic advantage in such a shamelessly pragmatic way.

Unlike resourcefully selfish figures such as Lucy Steele, Austen's heroines have a more passive relationship with the obstacles in their path. At times the only thing they can do about obstacles is idly wish them away. When the obstacle in question is a person, such wishes can take on a quasi-murderous bent. Lady Susan flippantly describes her old adversary Mr Johnson as 'too old to be agreable [*sic*], & too **young** to die' (*LM*: 62), but she is by no means the only Austen character to imagine that someone else's death would solve an awful lot of problems. Even sensitive and humane souls can't always help noticing how a timely demise might help clear a path towards happiness. There is a moment in *Sense and Sensibility*, for example, when Elinor Dashwood 'wished Willoughby a widower' (*SS*: 379). In *Emma*, the heroine reflects on 'how benefited, how freed' (*E*: 422) Frank Churchill will be when his aunt, who seems to exist purely to thwart her nephew's plans to come to Highbury, dies. No vengeful rancour or violent resentment characterizes these death-related thoughts in Austen. Rather, they tend to be floated as passing speculations about how things would look if the offending person were conveniently subtracted from things. A timely death is just the thing to release the blockage and let desire take its course.

When Austen's heroines aren't idly fantasizing about the destruction of obstacles they can develop perverse and melancholy attachments to them. 'Desire for the object', as Phillips points out, can mask 'desire for the obstacle' (1994: 82). Consider, for example, the feelings provoked in Elinor Dashwood by everything that separates her from Edward Ferrars. The first chapter of volume II of *Sense and Sensibility* finds the novel's thoughtful, long-suffering heroine 'mourning in secret over obstacles which much divide her for ever from the object of her love' (*SS*: 161). To be sure, there are plenty of reasons to believe that Elinor may be 'divided from Edward for ever' (*SS*: 299). Even if he wasn't already secretly engaged to Lucy Steele, their path to happiness is strewn with stumbling blocks, from Elinor's own comparative poverty to Edward's lack of personal, professional and financial independence, to the hostile attitudes and behaviour of his appallingly overbearing mother. In a context where the barriers between Elinor and the object of her desire are almost comically numerous and diverse, it seems possible that Austen's heroine may have become unconsciously attached to those very obstacles. It is as though she finds in the plight of distance and separation a source of emotions that are more exquisitely intense than anything married life with the uninspiringly tepid Edward Ferrars ever seems likely to provide.

There will often be a point in an Austen novel where the heroine, hemmed in by obstacles, can't see a way to happiness. With exquisitely cruel timing, Lydia's elopement with Wickham in *Pride and Prejudice* re-introduces and consolidates all the old barriers between Elizabeth and Darcy at the very moment when something like a relationship was developing between the two. The possibility that their nascent romantic understanding will survive this shameful episode seems somewhere between remote and non-existent. Part of the irresistible comic logic of *Pride and Prejudice*, however, is that it envisages obstacles as problems that become their own solutions. If Lydia had actively wanted to sabotage Elizabeth and Darcy's prospects of marriage then she would have had no better strategy than to run off with Darcy's old enemy. Yet the novel's principals will in the end have Lydia to thank for their marriage. If Lydia hadn't eloped with Wickham then Darcy would never have had the opportunity to intervene so magnanimously in the Bennet family's affairs. Darcy's rehabilitation and the novel's happy ending would be impossible without Lydia's debacle. The novel's most infuriatingly obstructive characters manage to bring off what its most enthusiastic matchmakers could never manage.

A principle of retrospective alchemy operates in *Pride and Prejudice*, where all the seemingly insurmountable obstacles to marriage – all the misunderstandings and separations that contrive to keep the principals apart – are transformed into that which, in the end, will enable the marriage to be achieved with satisfying perfection. But in all the festive euphoria of Austen's endings, there is often a subtly melancholy undertone, one that is associated with the narrative's sense of its own imminent evaporation. Consider, for example, the moment towards the very end of *Mansfield Park*, when Edmund Bertram realizes, or decides, that he loves Fanny Price. Edmund, long vexed by the obstacles that lie between him and Mary Crawford, can finally see before him a remarkably straightforward 'road to happiness'. At long last, there is 'nothing on the side of prudence to stop him or make his progress slow; no doubts of her deserving, no fears from opposition of taste, no need of drawing new hopes of happiness from dissimilarity of temper […] no difficulties behind, no drawback of poverty or parent' (*MP*: 544–5). Everything that might stand as a roadblock on the journey to happiness has vanished, if it was even there in the first place. As those obstacles melt away, so too does the narrative substance of *Mansfield Park*. What Edmund sees before him is a short, direct and frictionless path to happiness and fulfilment. It's a journey, of sorts – but it isn't a novel.

P IS FOR POOR

'How much are the Poor to be pitied, & the Rich to be blamed!' (*J*: 344). These words, written by the teenage Austen in the margins of her copy of Oliver Goldsmith's *History of England*, take an unusually forthright political stance on a subject about which her fiction is comparatively muted. Though her novels exhibit humane concern for the welfare of vulnerable people, they do not say much about the socio-economic causes of deprivation, or pose inconvenient questions about the gap between the poor and rich, or ask what it would take to live in a world without poverty. When Knightley remonstrates with the heroine of *Emma* about her cruelty to Miss Bates, he represents the poverty of the latter as a regrettable inevitability: 'She is poor; she has sunk from the comforts she was born to; and, if she live to old age, must probably sink more' (*E*: 408). For the novel's richest man, the progressive impoverishment of Miss Bates is a natural process that is as inescapable as ageing.

The comparative invisibility of the poor in Austen's writings is something that has long troubled her more politicized readers (Williams 1970; Aers 1981). Although she writes on seemingly universal experiences such as love, family and friendship, she does so within a sharply delimited range of class experience with a particular focus on the lives of respectable landowners and their families in provincial England. A typical Austen novel will be the story of how the daughter of a clergyman or landowner becomes the wife of a clergyman or landowner – it will be a story, in other words, of social consolidation in which the heroine acquires a more secure and enduring version of the respectable class position that she already occupied. If poverty and destitution are evoked, it will usually be in negative terms, as everything that our heroine has avoided by marrying well.

Not all readers believe that Austen is indifferent to the plight of the destitute. Despite the author's focus on a relatively affluent demographic, readers such as Sheryl Craig (2015) and David Wheeler (2003) have argued that her fiction is sympathetically attuned to the contemporary debates about poverty that would eventuate in the reform of the Poor Law in 1834.

Against a backdrop of financial crisis and economic decline, and at a time when the poor were routinely blamed for their own poverty, Austen attaches significant value to the acts of charitable **kindness** performed by figures such as Knightley and Darcy. Nor is poverty in Austen restricted to an anonymous, off-stage demographic known as 'the poor'. The stories of Austen's respectable-but-precarious heroines, from Catherine Morland to Anne Elliot, churn with unspoken financial anxiety.

According to Wheeler, the question 'who are the poor?' (2003: 147) is one that would in Jane Austen's lifetime significantly preoccupy moralists, economists and social commentators from Adam Smith to Thomas Malthus to Edmund Burke. Even in relation to the characters in Austen's fiction, this is not an easy question to answer. A glimpse of absolute poverty is offered by the sponging-house in *Sense and Sensibility* where Colonel Brandon **visits** a former **servant** who has been confined for debt – and where he finds the elder Miss Williams, penniless and wasting away with consumption. But 'poor' in Austen is not always synonymous with wretched destitution. The Watsons are introduced as 'poor' (*LM*: 79) even though they have servants and a **horse** and carriage (albeit old, decrepit ones). The heroine of *Lady Susan* is described as 'poor' (*LM*: 22) by Sir Reginald de Courcy, though what he means by this is that her husband had to sell his castle before he died. Poverty in these cases is more a direction of travel than a condition of living. In *The Watsons*, the heroine's father is in declining health and when he dies he will leave his unmarried daughters in significant financial difficulty. Lady Susan, if she doesn't re-marry advantageously, will not recover her old, privileged lifestyle. With the exception of Emma Woodhouse, the heroines of Austen's major novels all have to contend with the very real possibility that they will sink from the comforts they were born to. The fate of the Bennet sisters in *Pride and Prejudice* is deeply uncertain because Longbourn is entailed to Mr Collins and their father hasn't managed to set money aside to secure their future after his death. In *Persuasion*, Anne Elliot and her family seem to be set on a slow-motion journey of downward mobility. Poverty is the future that Austen's heroines don't want to think about.

Powerful taboos govern what Austen's heroines can and can't say about their own – frequently delicate – financial circumstances. The Jane Austen heroine can't ventilate anxiety about her economic vulnerability, still less can she be seen to work strategically and pro-actively to secure her future. Other characters, however, are free to vocalize what Austen's heroines can't say about money. In *Pride and Prejudice* Elizabeth Bennet is hardly a slave to convention or a demure idealist, but it is left to Charlotte Lucas to spell out the function of advantageous marriage as a safeguard against poverty. In *Sense and Sensibility*, Willoughby talks candidly to Elinor Dashwood about the way his pattern of selfish behaviour has been shaped by a certain 'dread of poverty' (*SS*: 366). We're not meant to sympathize with Willoughby here, or to regard his dread of poverty as any kind of exculpatory alibi for his callous behaviour to Marianne; even so, it is instructive to hear someone articulating so emphatically a fear that almost dare not speak its name in Austen's fiction. In her **letters**, she could be more candid. 'Single Women have a dreadful propensity for being poor', she writes to her niece Fanny Knight, 'which is one very strong argument in favour of Matrimony' (*L*: 347). These words disclose, with breezy candour and unapologetic pragmatism, all the unspoken financial anxieties that prey on Austen's heroines – but they are not words that any of those heroines would be permitted to say.

A keynote of Austen's response to poverty is fear. Ever since W. H. Auden joked about the 'amorous effects of brass' in her fiction, it has been a commonplace to suggest that money is the most potent aphrodisiac in her work. However, it is worth emphasizing that *not being poor* – as opposed to striking it rich – is the happy outcome that Austen's narratives most frequently ask us to celebrate. Elizabeth Bennet hits the jackpot when she marries Mr Darcy, but she is an exception. For heroines such as Catherine Morland, Elinor Dashwood and Fanny Price marriage is a reprieve from the implied threat of poverty rather than a passport to fabulous wealth. In the two Austen novels named after grand houses – *Northanger Abbey* and *Mansfield Park* – the heroine does not become mistress of the estate but rather of a nearby parsonage. The country house is a symbol of cultural value in Austen to the extent that it is not envisaged as a material prize. The Austen character who weds most advantageously – Maria Bertram, who becomes the mistress of Sotherton Court in *Mansfield Park* when she marries the tremendously wealthy James Rushworth – is the one whose marriage is most short-lived.

When poverty strikes in Austen, money drains away more quickly than respectability. Characters of limited financial means will continue to enjoy a degree of social recognition in privileged social worlds. The Watsons move in the same circles as the Edwardses, 'people of fortune' (*LM*: 79). Mrs and Miss Bates in *Emma* are on visiting terms with the Highbury elite. In *Persuasion*, the impoverished widow Mrs Smith can play host to Anne Elliot. For Austen's respectable poor, dealing with poverty is as much a psychological problem as an economic predicament. It helps if there are visibly poorer people in the neighbourhood. Miss Bates in *Emma* has John Abdy – 'Poor old John'

(*E*: 416) – to worry about. Mrs Smith in *Persuasion* makes handicraft items to do good by 'very poor families in this neighbourhood' (*P*: 168). Like those cartoon characters who can keep sprinting in mid-air after they have run off a cliff-edge, Austen's respectable poor find ways to defy gravity. Poverty can be held at bay for as long as you display enough selfless charity, neighbourly goodwill and noblesse oblige to sustain a reasonably dignified role-play enactment of the life and manners of the affluent person.

Whereas Austen displays considerable interest in the lives of the respectable poor, the 'very poor' – as Mrs Smith calls them – are evoked only in marginal and indirect ways. Frequently the poor feature in her work not as free-standing characters but as a measure of rich people's kindness and humanity. The revelation that Darcy does 'much good among the poor' (*PP*: 292) counts significantly towards his rehabilitation in the later stages of *Pride and Prejudice*. In *Mansfield Park*, Henry Crawford, eager to impress Fanny Price with his renewed moral seriousness, takes a philanthropic interest in the tenants on his Norfolk estate and makes himself 'the **friend** of the poor and oppressed!' (*MP*: 469). The difference between Darcy (whose concern for the poor is real) and Crawford (whose concern is cynically feigned) is clear enough. However, although Austen differentiates carefully between various kinds of relationship with the poor, her discerning gaze does not extend to the lived experience of the impoverished. The poor can tell us about Darcy and Crawford, but Darcy and Crawford can tell us nothing about the poor.

We seem to get a little closer to the lives of the impoverished when Emma Woodhouse pays a charitable visit to a 'poor sick family' (*E*: 89) who live a little way outside of Highbury:

> Emma was very compassionate; and the distresses of the poor were as sure of relief from her personal attention and kindness, her counsel and her patience, as from her purse. She understood their ways, could allow for their ignorance and their temptations, had no romantic expectations of extraordinary virtue from those, for whom education had done so little; entered into their troubles with ready sympathy, and always gave her assistance with as much intelligence as good-will.
>
> (*E*: 93)

Nowhere else in *Emma* does Austen's heroine seem to cut such an admirably selfless figure as in this sketch of her kindness, sympathetic understanding and generosity towards the poor of the parish. What makes this passage tricky to read, however, is its conspicuous reluctance to follow through on everything it praises in Emma. She visits the poor family's cottage, but the novel doesn't follow her in. Austen's imagination doesn't co-habit, even briefly, the lifeworld of Highbury's impoverished residents. Represented as pitiable abstractions – 'sickness and poverty together' – the members of this family have no names, no individuality, no history, no relationships with each other. Even as this episode raises complex questions about Emma's apparent generosity (would she even have been in this part of this village, so close to the Vicarage, if it wasn't conducive to her **matchmaking** plans for Harriet Smith and Mr Elton?), it also causes us wonder about the limits to the imaginative generosity of Austen's writings.

Emma's charitable visit to the cottage on Vicarage Lane provides a useful insight into what we can call the topography of poverty in Austen's writings. Just as her novels engage thoughtfully with the topical question 'who are the poor?', so they also raise the related question '*where* are the poor?'. Poverty, in her fiction, tends to have its own designated marginal spaces. The main events will usually take place on a grand estate or in an elegant townhouse, privileged vantage-points from which we will occasionally glimpse humble cottages and their variously underprivileged or destitute inhabitants. In *Pride and Prejudice*, cottagers provide an audience and backdrop for Lady Catherine de Bourgh in all her officious majesty: 'whenever any of the cottagers were disposed to be quarrelsome, discontented or too poor, she sallied forth into the village to settle their differences, silence their complaints, and scold them into harmony and plenty' (*PP*: 190). In *Persuasion*, when Sir Walter departs for **Bath** the 'afflicted tenantry and cottagers' (*P*: 38) gather to receive his condescending farewell bows. Cottagers in these novels represent and embody a version of poverty that can be contained in picturesque spatial terms as a backdrop to the high-handed antics of the rich. We never go inside the cottages, and the cottagers themselves are granted no interiority – no significant or reportable inner life – by Austen's narratives.

There is one moment in Austen when poverty acquires all the voice, agency and identity that it normally lacks in her work. When Harriet Smith and Miss Bickerton in *Emma* come across a group of gypsies on the Richmond road they encounter a startlingly **unexpected** presence in a social world where the privileged like to dictate the terms of their relationship with the very poor. Straying beyond Austen's official topographies of poverty, the gypsies are unsettling precisely to the extent that they are unsettled. As they beg Harriet for money, they confront a representative of Austen's orderly social world with a version of poverty that is mobile rather than contained,

Q IS FOR QUEER

'[I]s she out, or is she not?' (*MP*: 56); 'Is she queer?' (*MP*: 268). These questions, which are posed about Fanny Price in *Mansfield Park*, have been increasingly applied to Austen herself in the light of modern queer theory. Queer theory is a strategy of reading that aims to question heterosexuality's position as the dominant, 'default' form of sexual identity and orientation, and to rescue 'nonstandard' sexual identities from obscurity and stigma. A queer reading of Austen is one that asks what her novels would look like if our readings weren't governed by heteronormative assumptions. A signature move of this kind of reading is a strategic use of anachronism. 'Queer', in Austen's time, signified 'odd' or 'peculiar'. The expression has been on quite a semantic journey since the early nineteenth century, and after a spell as a nasty homophobic slur it has been reclaimed and repurposed in the early twenty-first century as a catch-all term for identities and orientations that can't be easily assimilated to traditional, heterosexual norms. One significant wager of a queer reading of Austen is that there might be considerable value in letting ourselves hear this modern sense of 'queer' in her use of the word. Her whimsically experimental early work was described by her nephew as 'caring only for "the queerness and the fun"' (Austen-Leigh [1871] 2002: 43), and recent readers have had fun exploring the queerness of her writings. D. A. Miller, for example, has shown that her life and work can be read as a critique of the oppressiveness of 'omnipresent marriage culture' (1995: 4). As a successful unmarried woman, Austen stands outside and achieves some critical distance from the traditional culture of courtship and matrimony that her work officially celebrates.

One ambition of queer readings is to grant substance and visibility to the varieties of non-heterosexual identity that have so often, and in so many ways, been denied official existence or institutional validation. Once we go looking for queer characters in her writings, we find them everywhere. In a detailed commentary on the jewellery shop scene in *Sense and Sensibility*, (2003: 9–20), Miller notes that the foppish Robert Ferrars is seemingly more engrossed in the finer details of his design for an exquisite toothpick case than in the nearby presence of marriageable **young** women. Nor is Robert Ferrars the only example of what Miller calls the 'Unheterosexual' (2004: 16) in Austen's world. Lady Denham in *Sanditon*, who has buried two husbands, has been described by one critic as bringing 'wealthy lesbian vampirism' (Tuite 2002: 178) into Austen's fiction. In *Pride and Prejudice*, when Darcy and Wickham first bump into each other, they react with an extraordinarily strong mixture of embarrassment and anger. What lies behind this reaction? Would it be possible to speculate that Darcy responds to Wickham in the way he does because Wickham is his ex-? When two single men who used to be on intimate terms react so strongly to one another after years of separation but are evasive in different ways about the specifics of their shared history, it seems a fair question to ask. The queer reading of the Darcy/Wickham relationship is there, if you want to see it, to or write it, between the lines.

If there is one thing we know from Austen's representations of single men it is that they *must* – according to the most famous line she ever wrote – be in want of wives. But what is the force of 'must' in this sentence? Does it imply formal obligation (as in: 'You must turn yourself in to the police') or simple likelihood (as in: 'You must be my new neighbour?'). And how, if at all, is that 'must' enforced? Austen's fictions contain revealing depictions of the figure of the eligible but unattached person who resists the force of that *must* – the person who doesn't, for whatever reason, seem to be 'in want of' a life partner. Exemplary in this regard, as Erin Spampinato (2019) has shown, is Tom Bertram in *Mansfield Park*. Tom is Sir Thomas's eldest child, and the heir to the estate; he is a playboy and gadabout, unattached but seemingly indifferent to the single women in his sphere such as Fanny Price and Mary Crawford. As Sir Thomas disappointedly observes, 'matrimony makes no part of his plans or thoughts' (*MP*: 366). It is unusual in Austen for well-developed male characters not to be tidied into matrimony – or, at the very least, not to be perceived as actively interested in the opposite sex. In his capacity as 'master of the house' (*MP*: 144), Tom becomes in his father's absence a champion of the 'cause of pleasure' (*MP*: 151) and effects a kind of queering of Mansfield Park as a space of play and performativity in which official roles and identities can be suspended for as long as the paterfamilias is out of the country. Of all the pleasure-seeking young people who congregate at Mansfield Park, Tom is the only one who does not seem to harbour romantic feelings for any fellow members of his friendship group. Fanny likes Edmund, Julia likes Henry, Yates likes Julia, on so on, but Tom is romantically unaligned; he is the **friend** of everyone but partial to no one. For the master of Mansfield Park, that fact that his marriage-resistant son has lots of male friends – a 'hundred particular friends' (*MP*: 214) – is gravely disappointing behaviour. When friendship becomes an end in itself, rather than a cover for flirtation and courtship, then it calls into question the supposed naturalness and inevitability of heterosexual romance. As Spampinato's analysis shows, in the heteronormative world of *Mansfield Park* Tom is the queer hero of a distinctly 'unheterosexual' subplot.

Persuasion has its own story of resistance to marriage culture. Despite their apparent compatibility, the heroine's father and his friend Lady Russell 'did *not* marry, whatever might have been anticipated on that head by their acquaintance' (*P*: 5). When marriage is the obvious course of action or the path of least resistance, then the decision *not* to marry is deemed to be a puzzlingly wilful gesture. Sir Walter's 'continuing in singleness', the narrator remarks, 'requires explanation' (*P*: 5). 'Singleness' is a singular word in Austen – nowhere else in her writings does she use it – but it is a state that, again and again, needs accounting for. There is a point where not-being-married needs a story, or, at least, an alibi. Sir Walter's singleness is particularly intriguing in the light of the fact that he is often insistent about his indifference to women. '[O]nce, as he had stood in a shop in Bond Street, he had counted eighty-seven women go by, one after another, without there being a tolerable face among them' (*P*: 153). What are we to make of his extraordinary pickiness in the visual marketplace of **Bath**? Are we to assume that it will only be a matter of time before the right woman – let's say woman number eighty-eight – catches Sir Walter's hyper-fastidious **eye**? Or is it the case that he has found what he was looking for in the company of good-looking men, whether it's Admiral Croft (the 'best-looking sailor he had ever met with' [*P*: 34]), Mr Elliot ('better to look at than most men' [*P*: 152]), or Colonel Wallis, with whom he walks arm in arm under the admiring gaze, as he imagines it, of every woman who passes (*P*: 153)?

Austen's most complex exploration of the queer possibilities that are present within marriage culture occurs in *Emma*. The novel's early chapters focus on the heroine's insistence that she will never marry, and on her intimate female friendships: first, there is her former governess Miss Taylor (now Mrs Weston), with whom she lived 'together as **friend** and friend very mutually attached' (*E*: 3); then there is her friendship with Harriet Smith, 'a very pretty girl' whose 'beauty happened to be of a sort which Emma particularly admired' (*E*: 22). You don't have to go too far back in critical history to find readers responding in openly homophobic ways to the currents of same-sex desire and attraction that are right there on the surface in *Emma*. Modern queer theory has provided more thoughtfully analytical responses to the novel's depiction of same-sex friendship and desire. Tiffany Potter (1994) has shown how Emma's relationships with other women – particularly Harriet and **Jane** – are routinely downgraded, as though our heroine's choice of Knightley is a choice against, and a rejection of, intimate female relationships in favour of heteronormativity. Influential voices in the novel seem to throw their weight behind this very process. Knightley, for example, sternly insists that Emma's relationship with Harriet was an 'infatuation' (*E*: 64) that she needs to get over. Yet the voices of *Emma* by no means add up to a chorus of unanimous approval for heteronormative marriage. Critics of the 'marriage culture' that pervades and underwrites Austen's fiction may notice that they have an unlikely ally in the person of Mr Woodhouse, the hypochondriac widower who, as his daughter puts it, is 'no friend to matrimony' (*E*: 302). Knightley, meanwhile, explains patronizingly but revealingly to Mrs Weston that during her time at Hartfield her relationship with Emma was that of a submissive wife (*E*: 38). You wouldn't have singled out Mr Knightley as the one who will broach the notion of same-sex marriage in Austen. Admittedly, he does so as a throwaway conceit, but it is remarkable all the same to see the idea of same-sex marriage as momentarily *thinkable* in this novel – and articulated by none other than the novel's most influential spokesman for heteronormativity.

Queerness is remarkably – and often subversively – legible in Austen's writings but heteronormativity sometimes has the power to absorb it. Consider, for example, the impressively debonair figure cut by Henry Tilney in *Northanger Abbey*. A charming and slightly waggish conversationalist, Henry is well-read, likes to **dance** and is fluent in the conventionally female discourses of fashion and journal writing. With archly flirtatious self-deprecation, he even describes himself to Catherine as a 'queer, half-witted man' (*NA*: 19). We can recognize in Tilney an early instance of modern perceptions of gay male subjectivity as definitively witty, cultured and stylish. These are flattering perceptions, to be sure, but flattening ones also, since they implicitly disallow or eclipse other forms of gay male identity (that is, they exclude gay men who aren't witty or interested in fashion). In any case, Henry Tilney will over the course of the novel be 'outed' as a straight man who, as Jillian Heydt-Stevenson puts it, 'verbally cross-dresses so as to woo and patronize women' (2005: 20). Towards the end of Catherine's brisk guided tour of the Abbey, she and General Tilney pass through 'a dark little room, owning Henry's authority, and strewed with his litter of books, guns, and great coats' (*NA*: 188). This 'dark little room' seems to represent a hidden or underplayed side of Catherine's love interest.

In a remarkable moment of intimacy with the absent Henry, the books, the guns, the coats and perhaps above all the *mess* provide a glimpse, behind the polished fashionista of Bath, of the messy closet of his heterosexuality.

The case of Henry Tilney, the 'unheterosexual' straight love interest of *Northanger Abbey*, is one instance of the endlessly complex ways in which queerness and heteronormativity are entangled with one another in Austen's fiction. No writer is more formally committed than Austen to heteronormative values, yet no writer does a more deft job of showing heteronormativity making a fool of itself or intruding oppressively on those who persist in singleness or prefer same-sex attachments. Long after her experimental teenage writings, 'the queerness and the fun' continue to be definitive qualities of her work.

R IS FOR RISK

Opportunities for pleasure and exposure to risk are often part of the same experience in Austen. When **Jane** Bennet receives an invitation to **visit** the Bingleys, for example, the question arises of whether she would be better off visiting on horseback or by carriage. A journey on horseback will expose the eldest Bennet daughter to the uncertain weather – but, for this very reason, will enhance the likelihood that her stay at Netherfield, in the company of her admirer Charles Bingley, will be extended. What is potentially bad for Jane's health is potentially good for her chances of advantageous marriage. As she ponders this choice – or, rather, as Mrs Bennet ponders the choice on Jane's behalf – we can appreciate the extent to which Austen, though her novels might seem to be harmlessly confined to the comfort zones of elegant Regency sociability, is a purveyor of fundamentally *risky* narratives.

The act of coming out is the prototypical, necessary risk for all of Austen's heroines. To establish a social identity outside the family home is to make a kind of existential wager that the rewards will outweigh the hazards as you navigate a new landscape of uncertainty. Even seemingly trivial decisions – whom to spend time with, whom to **dance** with, whom to travel with – draw her heroines into complex reckonings around the risks and rewards of a given course of action. Austen's characters can risk their health (exposure to rain or cold weather leads to **illness** for Jane Bennet and Marianne Dashwood); their reputation (Marianne's intimacy with Willoughby exposes her to potentially scurrilous and harmful gossip); their economic security (Elizabeth Bennet has no guarantee of a better offer when she rejects Mr Collins's proposal); and their happiness (Anne Elliot risks a lifetime of regret when she says **no** to Wentworth). Moments of decision require the Austen heroine to draw on what piecemeal information she has at her disposal to weigh competing risks in time-sensitive contexts. When Charlotte Lucas accepts Mr Collins's proposal she trades happiness for economic security. When Harriet Smith says no to Robert Martin, she sacrifices the possibility of happy marriage to the more immediate pleasures of her friendship with Emma Woodhouse.

Recent critics have emphasized the ways in which Austen's fiction involves her heroines in sharply competitive struggles for advantage and survival. Michael Suk-Young Chwe reads Austen's novels as 'chronicles of how a **young** woman learns strategic thinking skills' (2013: 49) – that is, the ability to make complex choices informed by a sense of what others may be thinking. Effective strategic thinking, Chwe contends, will lead to 'payoff maximization' (2013: 11). For Julia Hoydis, Austen's fiction displays a 'pre-Darwinian interest [...] in mechanisms of adaptation and survival' (Hoydis 2019: 254). Such perspectives are valuably thought-provoking even if the idiom in which they are couched is comically remote from Austen's own literary voice. It seems incongruous to invoke the notion of 'payoff maximization' when we ask if Jane Fairfax is wise to go to the post office in the rain to collect her mail. But the risk of exposure to the elements is not a trivial one for a character with uncertain health; and neither is the risk of exposure to gossip and speculation for a character with secrets to keep. What is more, those hazards must be weighed against the emotional risk of missing a **letter** from Frank Churchill. There is no risk-free course of action for Jane. Nor, for Austen's heroines, are there ever any risk-free courses of *inaction*. As Fanny Price discovers in *Mansfield Park*, even a scrupulous policy of doing nothing – not joining in, not acting, not accepting Henry Crawford's suit of marriage – has its own considerable risks.

Jane Fairfax's visits to the post office are one example of how Austen's fiction asks its heroines to weigh up painfully delicate risks associated with what might seem like the most inconsequential everyday matters. On the face of it, there is a fairly stark gendering of risk in her novels. Whereas the Austen heroine might agonize over, say, accepting a social invitation, male characters are often exposed to physical danger, sometimes in life-or-death situations. Not that Austen ever gives us a ringside seat at these episodes of risky physical drama. It's extraordinary to think how little *Sense and Sensibility* makes of the fact that two of its main characters – Willoughby and Brandon – fight a duel with each other. In *Persuasion*, we don't see any naval battles although Wentworth soon realizes that he has a captive audience of female admirers for his tales of adventure at sea. Austen's heroines, by contrast, are risk-takers who are obliged to behave as though they are impeccably cautious. Elizabeth Bennet takes considerable risks when she rejects Collins, who would have made her comfortable, and Darcy, who would have made her rich. Typically, however, she downplays any riskiness associated with her decisions. 'I am not one of those young ladies', she says to Collins, '[...] who are so daring as to risk their happiness on the chance of being asked a second time' (*PP*: 120). Anne Elliot's story in *Persuasion* has been described by E. J. Clery as one that is emphatically on the side of risk (2017: 279) but this is a quality that the novel's heroine scrupulously downplays. When Anne is finally and permanently re-united with Captain Wentworth, she says that if she had been wrong to reject him first time round it was in yielding to persuasion 'on the side of safety, not of risk' (*P*: 266). The Austen heroine can't not take risks – but she can't be seen to embrace or enjoy them.

A certain puritanical distaste for gambling hovers over Austen's representations of risk. It has been said that England in the eighteenth century was in the grip of 'gambling fever' (Porter 1982: 225), and outbreaks of this fever are occasionally visible in her fiction. In *Mansfield Park*, Tom Bertram's feverish love of gambling prefigures the actual fever that will nearly claim his life. In *Pride and Prejudice*, the news that Mr Wickham is a 'gamester!' (*PP*: 328) helps to place him emphatically beyond the pale of respectability. Gambling is problematic in Austen not simply because it is risky but because it fosters a certain enjoyment of risk for its own sake. To the extent that Austen moralizes about risk she does so against recklessly irresponsible pleasure in risk – especially when the risk is outsourced to other people. One thing that makes Emma Woodhouse's misadventures in the field of **matchmaking** so problematic is that they seem almost entirely risk-free for Austen's heroine. Harriet Smith's happiness is at stake when she receives a proposal from Robert Martin but comparatively little is at stake for Emma as she guides the choices of her naïve protégée. Emma, by virtue of her wealth, partakes of a privilege that is mostly restricted to men in Austen – that is, the privilege of swaggering or mischievous enjoyment in risk.

The very mention of gambling can send a quiver of moral indignation through Austen's prose, but such puritanical attitudes don't seem to apply to card games such as lottery tickets (*Pride and Prejudice*) or speculation (*Mansfield Park*), which are represented in her fiction as fairly harmless diversions, albeit ones that can symbolically disclose a lot about the players and their social world (Selwyn 1998: 265–75). The low-stakes recreational jeopardy of card games in Austen is nothing to worry about because its potentially dangerous effects – aggressive competitiveness, a self-destructive addiction to risk for its own sake – are decently mitigated and contained by the robust structures of family life. The four walls of the respectable gentry household can comfortably withstand the anti-social potentialities of gambling.

The gambling that excites moral horror in Austen is the gambling that happens *elsewhere* – at the race-track, the gaming house or the gentlemen's club. Beyond the perimeters of respectable village life in her world are risky, enticing spaces such as **Bath**, Ramsgate and Brighton, hubs of sociability that offer the promise of fun and novelty but also the risk of seduction and betrayal. To borrow a term from Elaine Freedgood, the watering-spaces and seaside resorts of Austen's fiction occupy a distinctive position in what we can call the author's 'geography of risk' (2000: 1) – that is, her mental map of the places of safety and danger in a given culture. One way of containing and mitigating risk – or, rather, one way of *imagining* that we can contain it – is to point to it on a map, to identify it is as endemic to a seamy and disreputable place that is a good way from home. As Freedgood points out, the appeal – and the inherent problem – of geographies of risk is that they offer a spatial solution to a temporal problem. If risk can be located anywhere, it is not at this or that location on the map but rather in the future – whether it's a moment or a lifetime from now. In the absence of reliable maps of the future, Austen's geographies of risk provide her fiction with a deceptive sense of reassurance in the face of inescapable uncertainty. So long as the truly reckless risks are happening elsewhere – in Bath, say, or Brighton – then the country house can feel reassured of its own impregnable security.

A more radical way of managing risk is to try to eliminate it from your life. It is in the ranks of Austen's influential older characters that we will find the strongest advocates of a zero-tolerance approach to risk. In *Persuasion*, the counsel of Lady Russell, who is instrumental in convincing Anne Elliot to reject Wentworth's proposal, is shaped by her horror of 'any thing approaching to imprudence' (*P*: 29). But Lady Russell is an absolute daredevil when compared to Mr Woodhouse in *Emma*. Few characters in the history of literature have been more pathologically risk-averse than Emma's father. Mr Woodhouse can see danger everywhere. Eating a slice of wedding cake, dancing through a draughty passage, hovering near an open window, making a short journey to see neighbours – all of these are, by his reckoning, unconscionably risky activities. With his capacity to discern peril in food, drink, motion, dance and the weather, it is as though he regards the very substance of an Austen novel as radioactive with danger. While Austen deplores the gambler's reckless enjoyment in risk, she perceives something no less troubling in the way Woodhouse, the anti-gambler par excellence, obtains perversely fretful enjoyment from his own fear of risk.

Mr Woodhouse is a memorable case study in the psychology of risk-aversion, but he is also a representative or historically exemplary figure, a doddery personification of an old feudal order that is beginning to lose its supremacy in the modern world. If we were looking for a precise antitype to Mr Woodhouse in this regard, we would point to Mr Parker, the entrepreneurial hero of *Sanditon*. Whereas Mr Woodhouse stands for an ancient system in which wealth, privilege and status are inherited, Parker is a creature of a new world of investment and speculation where fortunes can be made and lost overnight. This would have been a subject close to Austen's heart when she began work on *Sanditon*, given that Austen, Maunde and Tilson, the banking business of her brother Henry, collapsed the year before she began writing the novel (see Clery 2017: 265–75). Austen herself, as Clery points out, was not simply an artist but also a businesswoman who retained copyright of her published novels (with the exception of *Pride and Prejudice*) at the risk of remaining liable for any losses (Clery 2017: 140–1). *Sanditon* is the novel in which Austen most explicitly positions her social worlds in the context of emerging economies of risk. Whatever Parker's personal failings and eccentricities as a businessman, there is no question that he represents the emergence of a new economic system that will come into its own as the eighteenth-century squirearchy gives way to a new generation of investors, speculators and property developers, the risk-taking entrepreneurs of nineteenth-century capitalism. Again and again, Austen's fiction centres reassuringly on a once-precarious heroine who, by marrying well, can look forward to a future without risk. In the speculative commercial world of her last piece of fiction, however, risk is the future.

S IS FOR SERVANT

Austen's characters can't do without their servants – their cooks, maids, nannies, grooms, coachmen, housekeepers, gardeners and butlers. The servants are characters too, of course, albeit in restricted and diminished ways. We never really get to know the people in her novels who light the fires, prepare the food, manage the houses, maintain the gardens, run errands, deliver messages, supervise the **children**, look after the **horses**, clean the clothes and arrange transport of persons and property. With so much work on their hands, it maybe no surprise that the servants in Austen don't have the opportunity to come into their own as characters with inner lives, backstories or significant experiences outside of the domestic workplace. Defined by function rather than by individuality, the servant 'vanishes into the duty he or she performs' (Woloch 2003: 120). But they don't vanish without trace. A number of critics (Terry 1988; Walshe 2014; Dredge 2020) have dwelt thoughtfully on the marginal lives of domestic staff in Austen, while some novelists – Jo Baker's *Longbourn* (2014) is an outstanding recent example – have granted Austen's servants full-bodied storylines of their own.

Sometimes, when Austen's servants 'vanish', they do so into spectacular visibility. The social function of the liveried postillion in *Northanger Abbey* (*NA*: 159) or the doorman with a powdered head in *The Watsons* (*LM*: 88) is precisely to make a splendid visual impression. There are also moments when servants make their presence felt simply because there are so many of them, as in the case of John and Fanny Dashwood's grand dinner in *Sense and Sensibility*, where 'the servants were numerous, and every thing bespoke the Mistress's inclination for shew, and the Master's ability to support it' (*SS*: 265). In such contexts, servants are visible but only as voiceless extras, ornaments to the splendour of their households. From time to time, Austen will let us catch a glimpse of a servant who isn't wholly defined by their household function. The most divertingly human moments of Catherine Morland's rather exhausting tour of Northanger Abbey are her tantalizing sightings of off-duty servants: 'Wherever they went, some pattened girl stopped to curtsey, or some footman in dishabille sneaked off' (*NA*: 189–90).

Little though she dwells on it, Catherine's glimpse of a half-dressed footman is a revealing moment in a novel much concerned with her attempts to gain visual access to a hidden side of the Abbey, to see what she's not supposed to see. Off-duty servants provide her with a humanized and individualized glimpse of the inner workings of the class system as it underpins the seamless grandeur and elegance of the Tilney household.

The brief encounter with off-duty servants in *Northanger Abbey* is representative of the general rule in Austen that servants' appearances are fleeting and self-contained – there are servants in the story but the story is never about the servants. The behaviour and opinions of domestic staff tend to count only when they might provide insight into their masters. In *Sense and Sensibility*, servants provide a joyful welcoming committee for Mrs Dashwood and her daughters on their arrival at their new home in Devon (*SS*: 33). In *Pride and Prejudice*, the Pemberley housekeeper, Mrs Reynolds, gives superlatively glowing reports of Darcy – 'the best landlord, and the best master' (*PP*: 276) – that flatly contradict his reputation for insufferable haughtiness. The servant's-**eye** view of key characters has a special authority and authenticity in Austen because servants know her protagonists routinely, intimately and outside of the politely choreographed world of fashionable sociability. The 'authority of a servant' (*PP*: 292), in such contexts, really counts.

You can tell a lot about a character in Austen by asking whether they are on good terms with the servants. In *Mansfield Park*, where Mrs Norris is often bad-temperedly at odds with the Bertrams' staff, there's no question that our sympathies are with servants. In the same novel, no one emerges more unfavourably from Mrs Price's endless grievances about her servants than Mrs Price herself. None of this, it has to be said, amounts to anything like class consciousness in Austen's representation of social hierarchies. She champions the servants only to the extent that their perspectives corroborate what she wants to tell us about her central characters. The domestic staff who work in the various households of Austen's fiction have an all-important secondary job as servants of her narrative methods.

When servants are splendidly visible in Austen it is normally a sign that things are going smoothly; when servants become a topic of conversation, it can be a sign that things are going wrong. Rebecca in *Mansfield Park* comes to life in the Price family's bitterly indignant reports of her slowness and incompetence (*MP*: 445). When problems arise in the Price household – when things don't happen on time or when the food isn't as good as it should be – then servants are singled out as the scapegoats.

In *Northanger Abbey*, General Tilney is mightily displeased when he learns that his servant William did not formally admit Catherine to their household. William – until Catherine speaks up on his behalf – **risks** losing his post for this tiny flaw in the seamless choreography of civilized domestic life.

When Austen's characters grumble about the reliability of servants, often the focus is on their linguistic or narrative reliability. Questions may be raised about their competence in cleaning the dishes or greeting and announcing visitors, but more unsettling ones are raised about their reliability as speakers and listeners. Servants in Austen are associated with loose talk, indiscretion and the leaking of sensitive private information into a public domain of rumour and chatter. In *Sense and Sensibility*, Colonel Brandon's plan to elope to Scotland with Eliza is betrayed by his cousin's maid (*SS*: 233). In the same novel, the mildly scandalous news of Marianne's **visit** to Allenham Court leaks out via Willoughby's groom (*SS*: 79). In *Mansfield Park*, when reports surface of Maria Rushworth's affair with Henry Crawford, it is via one of her maid-servants (*MP*: 521).

One great privilege of employing servants in a grand household is that they function as a human shield that protects a family from the demeaning drudgery of everyday life. But the human shield is also an intimate audience, one that has a ring-side seat on the personal lives of Austen's characters. Austen's respectable families are plagued by anxieties about servants knowing their private business. Much to her daughters' discomfort, Mrs Bennet in *Pride and Prejudice* cannot 'hold her tongue before the servants' (*PP*: 318). What shocks Mary Crawford most about Maria Rushworth's behaviour is not her infidelity but her manner of 'putting herself in the power of a servant' (*MP*: 526). Moments of crisis in Austen are often compounded by the possibility that servants may acquire some degree of narrative mastery over their employers. When Lydia writes to announce her elopement with Wickham, Elizabeth is dismayed at the prospect of servants knowing 'the whole story' (*PP*: 322). Even though she has warm words for the 'authority of a servant', Austen's fiction can view with trepidation the moment when servants become storytellers. At other times problems arise not when servants possess 'the whole story' but when they get hold of a garbled version of half a story. When the Dashwoods' manservant Thomas returns from Exeter, he reports that Mr Ferrars has married Lucy Steele (*SS*: 400–2). It's the news that Elinor has been dreading, but the Mr Ferrars in question turns out to be Robert, not Edward. Thomas's involuntary misreporting of the facts of Lucy Steele's marriage is a reminder that any family with servants has its own in-house team of unreliable narrators, poised to broadcast and garble their private business.

Servants' power, such as it is, is frequently associated with their spatial positioning. Domestic staff in Austen are often stationed in the vicinity of doorways. From the hapless William in *Northanger Abbey*, to the 'trollopy-looking maidservant' (*MP*: 435) who greets Fanny Price on the doorstep of her old home, to Hannah in *Emma* who wins praise for never banging doors (*E*: 7), domestic staff hover in and are defined by these threshold spaces. In some ways the doorway is an unenviable position, simultaneously inside and outside the house, part of the family but out in the cold. But it's a position not without its privileges. Servants in Austen have an important gatekeeping role. They safeguard the privacy of the household from unannounced or unwanted intrusions. They patrol and mediate the gateway between inside and outside, and wield the householder's power to filter would-be visitors. When the Watsons play host to Lord Osborne and Tom Musgrave, they are interrupted by their servant, Nanny, 'half opening the door and putting in her head' to ask on behalf of Mr Watson '"why he be'nt to have his dinner"' (*LM*: 116). Speaking from a half-opened door, Nanny occupies the liminal space in which we so often find Austen's servants. Her voice is liminal too, marked as it is with irregularities and contractions but invested with the formal authority of Mr Watson's request. This brief intervention from a servant will tell Lord Osborne and Tom Musgrave a lot about the Watsons' uncertain, precariously in-between social position.

It makes sense that servants, the people who make life so comfortable for Austen's well-heeled families, can also be the source of exquisite discomfort. If you have servants, you'll never have to think about mopping the floor or cleaning your clothes, but you will have to think about what the servants might be thinking and saying about you. For these reasons, fears and fantasies of servantlessness circulate in Austen. 'I do believe *those* are best off, that have fewest servants' (*LM*: 170) says Lady Denham in *Sanditon*. The mistress of Denham Park is not volunteering to do her own gardening or take care of the laundry; rather, she is ventilating a more general anxiety that in grand households there is sometimes more power-sharing between domestic staff and their employers than the latter might like to acknowledge. The practical reality of life without servants is another matter. In *Northanger Abbey*, when Catherine is expelled from the Tilney household, she has no servant with her on the seventy-mile journey home from Gloucestershire to Fullerton. No other Austen heroine makes such a long journey unaccompanied. It's a kind of final examination for Catherine, one in which a character so prone to daydreaming and fantasy proves she has the good sense and practical nous to navigate a difficult cross-country journey without assistance. To make such a journey without a servant – without someone who would have combined the roles of personal assistant, baggage handler and de facto bodyguard – is greatly to her credit. But, now that she has passed this particular test, it is not something that she will ever have to do again.

Nothing about Austen's servants provokes more vexation than the suspicion that they might be enjoying themselves. In *Persuasion*, Mary Musgrove insists that her mother-in-law's servants are 'gadding about the village, all day long' (*P*: 48); Mrs Musgrove in turn alleges that Mary's nursery maid is 'always upon the gad' (*P*: 49). In *Mansfield Park*, Rebecca ruins Mrs Price's Sunday when the latter sees her 'pass by with a flower in her hat' (*MP*: 473). Memorably glimpsed here is a carefree Rebecca outside the household, dressed up, enjoying herself and for once undefined by servitude. In *Northanger Abbey*, Catherine Morland feels the need to remind herself that 'servants were not slaves' (*NA*: 205). Austen's characters also need the occasional reminder that servants are not servants – their humanity exceeds the household roles in which they are too glibly defined.

One of the most memorable expressions of pleasure from a servant in Austen is a smile. In *Mansfield Park*, when the butler Baddeley announces to Fanny that Sir Thomas wants to see her, Mrs Norris is unable to believe that *she* is not the object of the summons. Baddeley quietly makes it clear to Mrs Norris that she is in the wrong. His words are delivered with 'a half smile […] which meant, "I do not think *you* would answer the purpose at all"' (*MP*: 375). That 'half smile' is an extraordinarily rare thing in Austen, a sighting of a servant's inner life, a world of private emotion that is normally hidden behind a mask of dutiful efficiency. We don't quite know to read the smile, nor can we say with certainty whether the perception of the smile as a kind of smirk at Mrs Norris's expense is one that comes from Mrs Norris, or from Fanny, or from the narrator.

Baddeley's enigmatic half-smile is one instance of the curious sense of *halfness* that is repeatedly associated with Austen's servants. Rebecca serves up her inedible cooking on 'half-cleaned plates' with 'not half-cleaned knives and forks' (*MP*: 479). For Mrs Price things are so bad with servants that 'it is quite a miracle if one keeps them more than half-a-year' (*MP*: 445). In one particularly martyrous mood, she insists that she often has to 'do half the work' herself (*MP*: 445). Austen's respectable families need and rely on their servants even if they are continually provoked and annoyed by these half-dressed purveyors of half-finished jobs who deliver half-truths

T IS FOR THEATRE

'[W]hat signifies a theatre?' (*MP*: 145), asks Henry Crawford, when the **young** people of Mansfield Park are contemplating some amateur theatricals while the master of the house, Sir Thomas Bertram, is away on business in the **West Indies**. It's a calculatedly nonchalant question, one designed to play down the spatial impact – not to mention the potentially unseemly and risqué significance – of what's being proposed. But the implied answers to Henry's question are potentially troubling. A place for acting need only be a temporary, pop-up structure. A few simple changes are all that's needed to convert a domestic environment into a playhouse. A theatre can be anywhere. If 'theatre' amounts to a handful of temporary alterations, all easily disassembled and reversed, leaving no permanent trace in the substance of the house, then those who are alarmed by the prospect of play-acting in Mansfield Park seem to have nothing to worry about. But it is precisely the airy nothingness of 'theatre' – its rootlessness, mobility, impermanence and insubstantiality – that sows doubt in *Mansfield Park* about the authenticity and trustworthy of dramatic performance.

Not that Austen herself is by any means a dogmatically anti-theatrical writer. Her interest in drama and affection for the theatre is well-documented (Gay 2002: 1–25). Household theatricals, presided over by her brothers Henry and James and held in the barn in Steventon, were a significant part of her childhood. Her earliest writings include short dramatic comedies such as 'The **Visit**' and 'The Mystery'. When she was older she became a keen theatre-goer in **Bath**, London and Southampton. Key scenes in *Northanger Abbey* take place at the theatre. With its emphasis on showing through dialogue rather than intrusive telling, her style has important affinities with the dramatic method (Honan suggests that the dialogue of *Pride and Prejudice* is a bit *too* theatrical [1987: 309]). But Austen's affection for theatre co-exists, always, with a certain suspicion of theatricality. Often she plays half-jokingly with the prejudice that actors can't quite be trusted. In 'Love and Freindship', the heroine's cousins Gustavus and Philander carve out a successful career in acting after stealing and squandering 900 pounds from their mothers. The switch from thievery to theatricality is all too seamless. Her mature work takes more seriously the hunch that good actors – Willoughby in *Sense and Sensibility*, Henry Crawford in *Mansfield Park* – are bad people. Crawford declares his willingness to 'undertake any character that ever was written' (*MP*: 145), but it's hard to trust someone who can step so readily and convincingly out of his own skin. You can't help suspecting that a figure with such a limitless repertoire of possible roles is a shape-shifting nonentity rather than a knowable person.

In *Northanger Abbey*, which is in part a novel about whether you can ever really know other people, theatre has an important thematic role to play. The theatre in Bath is a social hub, a place to see and be seen, where the crowd itself is part of the spectacle. When Catherine Morland goes to the theatre we learn almost nothing about the content or nature of the plays being performed. A performance of a comic play holds her attention for the first four acts until she notices Henry Tilney and his father taking their places in a box opposite her. Visits to the theatre in *Northanger Abbey* are always dramatic, but not because of what's going on on-stage. Theatricality in the Bath-set fictions spills out from the stage, beyond the confines of the playhouse and into the streets and houses of the town itself, where the performative deceptions of role-players such as Isabella Thorpe or William Elliot are unmasked only after they have done much damage. In Bath, all the town's a stage.

Already perceptible in *Northanger Abbey* is the shift from theatre (the space earmarked for dramatic performance) to theatricality (the principle of performativity that pervades all human conduct) that Joseph Litvak (1992: 332) traces in Austen's most drama-obsessed novel, *Mansfield Park*. A significant portion of *Mansfield Park* concerns preparations for the staging of a work by the novelist and playwright Elizabeth Inchbald, a risqué melodrama entitled *Lovers' Vows* (1798). Itself a free adaptation of August von Kotzebue's *Das Kind der Liebe* (1780), *Lovers' Vows* is chosen for performance by the Bertram and Crawford siblings and their **friends**, a clique whose bored, frisky antics flourish in the vacuum created by Sir Thomas's absence. As numerous critics have remarked, the plot of *Lovers' Vows*, a far-fetched tale of family reunion and moral rehabilitation which ripples with flirtation and sexual impropriety, holds up a revealing mirror to unspoken currents of desire that criss-cross the friendship group assembled at Mansfield Park (see Tanner 2007: 164–5). When Mary Crawford and Edmund Bertram take on the roles of Amelia and Mr Anhalt, Mary gets to play the role of a young woman who flirts shamelessly with a very proper clergyman. Maria Bertram and Henry Crawford discover in the roles of Agatha and her long-lost son Frederick plenty of reasons to spend intimate time with one another. The man whom Maria will eventually discard in Crawford's favour, Mr Rushworth, might have seen his fate coming if he'd reflected on the significance of his role as the dim and resistible fop Count Cassel.

Revived in *Mansfield Park* is the old question of whether we can ever really trust those who have a flair for acting. When Henry Crawford reads from Shakespeare's *Henry VIII* – 'The King, the Queen, Buckingham, Wolsey, Cromwell, all were given in turn' (*MP*: 389) – his casual virtuosity is indicative of a freewheeling, opportunistic changeableness that can make his desires and intentions unknowable. Whether Crawford is acting or in earnest when he says he is in love with Fanny Price is impossible to say. One promise he makes Fanny is that there will never be a theatre at his home, Everingham (*MP*: 392), but such a promise is beside the point when he brings theatricality with him wherever he goes. Nor are the novel's scruples about acting restricted to the relatively simple point that acting masks an authentic self. Acting in *Mansfield Park* is a seductively dangerous experiment with the performance of identity and desire where a plunge into fiction may unlock unspoken truths. The rehearsal for *Lovers' Vows* requires cast members to feign emotions that they already feel, to simulate a sense of attraction to their real objects of desire. Edmund, acting opposite Mary Crawford, is caught 'between his theatrical and his real part' (*MP*: 191) while Maria Rushworth, acting opposite Henry Crawford, 'acted well – too well' (*MP*: 193).

The theatrics at Mansfield Park are remarkable for their concrete impact on the physical space of the Bertram household as well as on the mindsets of its inhabitants and visitors. When plans for acting are being hatched, Edmund initially maintains a guarded distance: 'If we are to act', he sarcastically declares, 'let it be in a theatre completely fitted up with pit, box, and gallery' (*MP*: 145). Nothing so extreme is undertaken, but the physical transformation of the house is nevertheless considerable. The billiard-room is re-purposed as '*the Theatre*' (*MP*: 161), while Sir Thomas's study becomes the green room. Furniture is moved around and domestic space is transformed by carpentry work and green curtains. Before too long, people are 'rehearsing all over the house' (*MP*: 198). Theatricality even finds its way to Fanny's rooms, the very headquarters of anti-theatricality in the Bertram household, when Edmund and Mary come to practise their lines. The performers are too wrapped up in the thrill of novelty to notice that it all feels mildly sacrilegious, although when Tom reassuringly declares that his father's house 'shall not be hurt' (*MP*: 149) he does implicitly acknowledge the **risk** that he and his friends may be perpetrating a symbolic and material injury to the fabric of Mansfield Park.

When Sir Thomas returns from Antigua he oversees an attempt to purge Mansfield Park of theatricality. The house is 'cleared of every object' (*MP*: 220) associated with the play. The carpenter dismantles the scenery, the painter is dismissed and – most hair-raisingly – copies of the script are tossed in the fire (*MP*: 223). It is as though Mansfield Park has had its own local revival of the old puritan embargo on theatre. The repressive crackdown on theatricality is formidable in its speed and severity but so sharply focused as to miss its prevalence in the social world of the novel. Sir Thomas's attempts to scrub every trace of theatricality from the household are a futile exercise in purification. The theatricals have an afterlife. Months after the event Mr Yates is still affectionately nicknamed Baron Wildenhaim (*MP*: 456). The rehearsals live fondly in the memory as a time when Mansfield Park came to life with 'employment, hope, solicitude, bustle' (*MP*: 262). Henry Crawford, meanwhile, will launch his own one-man show by pretending to be in love with Fanny Price – a pretence that *seems* to generate its own reality. Just because the theatre has been dismantled doesn't mean that theatricality has come to an end.

The conflict between Sir Thomas and the would-be actors is, in significant ways, an inter-generational battle. Theatre exerts special fascination, in this novel, on the young – that is, on those who do not yet inhabit fixed social roles as husbands, wives, parents or landowners. Play-acting is a way of enjoying freedom from not (yet) having a formal social identity – and, perhaps, delaying the moment when such an identity, with all its sobering duties and responsibilities, will be imposed. Such freedom from duty is not relished by the novel's heroine. 'I cannot act' (*MP*: 171), says Fanny, when she is asked to participate in the amateur theatricals. These three words amount to an enormously revealing self-portrait. Fanny cannot perform onstage because she has no dramatic experience, no aptitude or appetite for play-acting. In her meekly intransigent way, she cannot be other than herself. Nor, it seems, can she 'act' in the broader sense of the word. Her powers of choice and initiative are drastically limited in the world of the novel, though over time a certain kind of principled inactivity will become her forte. Despite her moral allergy to acting, Austen's heroine becomes an indispensable member of the troupe. Rehearsals are not long underway before her services are in demand as prompt, stage-hand, acting coach and general consultant. She knows the script of *Lovers' Vows* more or less off by heart and is pressed into understudying for Mrs Grant. Deeply reluctant to step onto the stage, she is drawn into the culture around it, the 'arrangements and dresses, rehearsals and jokes' (*MP*: 143), that is, to the off-stage world with all its excitable camaraderie. Yet, in the end, this off-stage world *is* the theatre. In a novel about a play that never happens, all the drama lies in the preparations for the drama: the choice of text, casting (with a lot of talk about who 'looks the part' [*MP*: 159]), costumes, rehearsals, the learning of lines, the construction of the playing space – not to mention the dynamics of flirtation, rivalry and infighting among the theatrical troupe.

Another way of understanding dramatic performance in this novel would be to insist that it *does* indeed take place, albeit outside of the theatrical space that was designed to contain it. The entire theatrical interlude at Mansfield Park, so briskly abandoned when Sir Thomas returns, has effectively been a 'rehearsal' for everything that happens later in the novel. In significant ways, the second half of Austen's novel *is* Inchbald's play as it has been cast and rehearsed at Mansfield Park. Not that Sir Thomas, as he busily incinerates copies of the play, will know this. If he had stifled his anti-theatrical prejudice and watched the play in performance he might have understood more fully than he does the emerging stories of desire and infidelity that are unfolding so damagingly in his family. The play happens despite – perhaps even because of – its own cancellation. Maybe the real tragedy of *Mansfield Park* is that Sir Thomas never gets to see *Lovers' Vows*.

U IS FOR UNEXPECTED

'[B]e sure to have something odd happen to you', Austen once wrote to Cassandra, 'see somebody that you do not expect, meet with some surprise or other' (*L*: 256). Nothing enlivens humdrum daily life as it is narrated in **letters** more than the intervention of unexpected novelty. The element of surprise is what redeems experience from routine, makes it story-worthy and shareable. That said, it's not immediately clear how Cassandra would act on her sister's whimsical and paradoxical advice. No one can plan their own surprises. But if she was looking for inspiration on the narrative powers and pleasures of surprise she might have done worse than go back to Jane's fiction. Austen's novels attach tremendous significance to what we don't see coming. A surprise can be a jarring **accident** (Louisa Musgrove on the steps at Lyme), a painfully funny coincidence (as when Sir Thomas walks in just when Mr Yates is ranting out his lines) or a startling turn-up (the news that Frank Churchill and Jane Fairfax are engaged). Nor is the value of the unexpected restricted to its pleasures as a trope. The capacity to be surprised, to be taken aback by the unexpected, is a healthy one. It's good to be ambushed by what we didn't foresee, what we don't yet understand. In *Northanger Abbey*, which has been described as a 'witty dissertation on surprise' (Miller 2015: 141), Catherine Morland is all too ready to be startled, to gasp at pre-imagined horrors, but her expectations, as Tave points out, are nearly always mistaken (1973: 38). Authentic surprise is that which, in exceeding foresight, causes us to re-think what we thought we knew, to reconsider how we process information, how we manage the limits of our knowledge. The unexpected in Austen is a healthily unpredictable antidote to everything that is 'foreseen and foreplanned' (*SS*: 313) by those in the grip of their own elaborate blueprints for the future. Forecasters in her fiction – those who, like Emma Woodhouse, believe they can see and shape the future – have a terrible track-record.

'I like unexpected pleasure' (*L*: 190), Austen wrote, in another letter to Cassandra. Her characters don't always share this fondness for the unexpected. 'Surprizes are foolish things' (*E*: 247) says Mr Knightley, with grand humourlessness, when Jane Fairfax unexpectedly takes delivery of the **gift** of a pianoforté in *Emma*. Knightley prides himself on his immunity and indifference to the unexpected. Those who delight in surprises, he implies, take a childish pleasure in novelty for its own sake, however trivial that novelty might be. Indeed, for Knightley, the very category of surprise is trivial and objectionable, irrespective of the 'content' of this or that particular surprise. Surprises are foolish because they make fools of us – or, to put it another way, they are potentially humiliating moments of epistemological vulnerability. They confront us with the limits of our ability to understand our world and what it might have in store for us. But who would want to live in a world without surprises? Knightley's brother John, himself something of a veteran killjoy, seems to inhabit just such a world. Heading off to a Christmas Eve dinner at Randalls, he glumly predicts that there will be 'nothing to say or hear that was not said and heard yesterday, and may not be said and heard again to-morrow' (*E*: 122). When John Knightley chafes at everything that is claustrophobically routinized and predictable in Highbury sociability, it is not because he craves novelty and variety. Rather, in his jaded unsurpriseability, he can't believe that people could be so hopelessly addicted to the recycled banalities of village gossip and dinner-party chatter. A different, more qualified kind of resistance to surprise is offered by the novel's heroine. Emma Woodhouse is fond of surprises but likes to think of them as things that happen to other people. When news breaks of Miss Taylor's engagement to Mr Weston, she prides herself on having seen, all along, what was going to happen; indeed, she was the person who can claim responsibility for bringing it about. Present circumstances are imaginatively reverse-engineered by *Emma*'s heroine as outcomes of her desires and intentions. She is Highbury's resident historian who poses as its infallible soothsayer.

Surprise brings with it a sense of shock that can be both disruptive and creative. When Sir Thomas walks in on Mr Yates, mid-speech, the latter gives 'perhaps the very best start he had ever given in the whole course of his rehearsals' (*MP*: 213). This moment of surprise is exemplary in its staging because of the impact of its disruptive unexpectedness on the written and rehearsed reality of drama. Sir Thomas's early homecoming is startling because it was never in the script. When Austen refers to Yates's *start* she uses the term in the sense of 'startle' rather than in the sense of 'initiate' or 'begin'. But *start* and *startle* have always been semantically linked and Austen's fiction implies that a surprise can indeed be the start of something new. Surprise can be an opportunity to be jolted out of defensive postures and established attitudes. In *Pride and Prejudice*, the shock waves of astonishment between Darcy and Elizabeth when they meet at Pemberley seem to generate the possibility that they can re-negotiate their relationship. In *Emma*, Frank Churchill's unpredictable appearances and interventions have the potential to rouse a torpidly uneventful village from its slumbers.

It's worth noting that Frank wouldn't be able to pull off the kind of surprises he specializes in if he wasn't a man. Surprising behaviour in Austen is performed and received in ways that are consistently shaped by assumptions about gender. Her male characters are often fond of perpetrating elaborate or mischievously attention-seeking surprises. Edward Stanley, in 'Catharine, or the Bower', likes to breeze into people's lives at unexpected moments, as when he comes uninvited to the Dudleys' ball, where he delights in the ripple of 'repetition of pleasure, Surprise, and Explanations' (*J*: 275) around his social movements. Tom Musgrave in *The Watsons* loves to 'take people by surprise, with sudden **visits** at extraordinary seasons' (*LM*: 126), as though to proclaim his own freedom from the tyranny of conventional social timetables.

Privileged male characters in Austen have a narcissistic habit of glorying in the permanent 'surprise' of their own presence in social spaces over which they already preside. They seek to win admiration for their charming insouciance – and to provoke envy for their ability to dictate the terms of their own social availability. When Austen's female characters spring surprises, on the other hand, they **risk** controversy and censure. Lady Catherine de Bourgh doesn't expect spirited backchat from Elizabeth Bennet. Neither Collins nor Darcy expects to be rejected by Elizabeth. When Henry Crawford proposes to Fanny Price and Mr Elton to Emma, they are confident of their chances of success. Marriage proposals come out of the blue, but the female **no** is the great counter-surprise in Austen's narratives.

As a novelist, Austen gets to wield the power of the unexpected in ways that would never be available to her heroines. As a narrative resource, however, surprise is easily cheapened and depleted. Surprise isn't surprising if it is too obviously and formulaically part of a novelist's storytelling methods. Fiction has to find new ways to defeat our expectations. Bruce Stovel (1989) has shown how *Pride and Prejudice* is constructed around a series of 'pseudo-surprises' followed by a series of genuine ones. The former are events by which the book's characters, but not its alert readers, are taken aback (as when Charlotte Lucas marries Mr Collins or Darcy proposes to Elizabeth); the latter are events that even the reader doesn't see coming (as when Elizabeth and Darcy stumble across one another at Pemberley).

Stovel's reading of *Pride and Prejudice* is widely applicable to Austen. Emma is shocked when Mr Elton proposes, but everyone – characters and readers alike – is shocked when word gets out that Frank Churchill and **Jane** Fairfax are engaged. What's shocking here is not the relationship itself but the fact that we have somehow contrived not to notice it for several hundred pages. Having satirized its know-it-all heroine for her faulty predictions and wayward misreadings, the novel confronts us with our own readerly limitations. It's hard to moralize about Emma's off-beam 'prophesies' (*E*: 152) when our own sense of the future has been so elaborately confounded. The novel's very structure cautions us against replicating the heroine's smug one-upmanship by obliging us to repeat her mistakes.

'When are calculations ever right?', Austen breezily wonders in a letter to Cassandra. 'Nobody ever feels or acts, suffers or enjoys, as one expects!' (*L*: 143–4). There is, however, a limit to which Austen's novels are governed by unexpectedness. In *Sense and Sensibility*, Elinor Dashwood is 'surprised and not surprised' (*SS*: 380) when she learns that Colonel Brandon is in love with her sister Marianne. 'Surprised and not surprised' is precisely the double and contradictory response that Austen's narratives of the unexpected are designed to provoke. Her storylines are surprising – often escalatingly so – until we reach the non-surprise of the ending. You don't have to share Emma Woodhouse's divinatory self-confidence to guess an Austen novel will end in a happy marriage, even if the journey to that conclusion might contain plenty of **zigzags** along the way. Any doubt or unpredictability attaches to the *how* rather than the *what* of the final outcome. The specifics of that outcome might be temporarily startling (Frank and Jane!) but no one is going to be flabbergasted by the news that an unattached man is engaged to an unattached woman of comparable rank and status. The story of a novel such as *Emma* works with the force of surprise, but works also to contain it, to harness its power to tradition and convention. In Austen's tales of the unexpected, nothing is more wonderfully surprising than the status quo.

V IS FOR VISIT

In November 1813, Austen's brother Edward went to inspect Canterbury Gaol in his capacity as a visiting magistrate. Jane went with him, and reported to Cassandra that she 'went through all the feelings which People must go through I think in visiting such a Building' (*L*: 258). This **letter** provides a remarkable glimpse of Austen in what could scarcely be a less Austen-like setting – the author of *Pride and Prejudice* in the world of *Little Dorrit*. The prison-visitor experience does not however seem to have furnished her with any direct inspiration for her fiction. The only prisons in her works are figurative ones – the 'dismal old prison' (*MP*: 62) of Sotherton Court in *Mansfield Park*, for example, or the **Bath** that Anne Elliot wants to escape in *Persuasion*. The practice of visiting is, nevertheless, absolutely central to her writings. Frequently adopting a visitor's-**eye** view of society, her fiction examines the terms on which visitors enter and exit grand households and meditates on the power, pleasure and responsibilities that are attached to the visitor role.

There isn't an Austen novel that doesn't engage with the experience of spending time as a guest in other people's houses. Visiting, for many of her heroines, is the closest thing they have to a job. Her most well-known novel, *Pride and Prejudice*, is the story of its heroine's brief but hectically eventful career as perpetually mobile, in-demand visitor. Elizabeth Bennet spends time as a house-guest with Charles Bingley at Netherfield; with her aunt Phillips at Meryton; with her aunt and uncle, the Gardiners, on Gracechurch Street in London; and with Mr Collins and Charlotte at Hunsford in Kent – where she is also hosted by Lady Catherine de Bourgh at Rosings. During a tour of Derbyshire, she is shown round Pemberley in Mr Darcy's absence, and later receives an **unexpected** invitation from Darcy himself to visit his family seat. The novel ends when the whirl of visiting ends – that is, when Elizabeth Bennet is no longer defined by the visitor role.

Pride and Prejudice traces one possible map of the routes via which unmarried **young** women can circulate through the respectable households and social spaces of Georgian society. Like so much of Austen's art, this novel reflects on the art of visiting and of receiving visitors that is so indispensable to the culture of sociability among the landed gentry, a social world where formal invitations and impromptu calls provide a steady supply of guests for the best households (see: McMaster 1995: 47–58; Selwyn 1998: 10–16). Visiting in Austen is a pleasurable and recreational activity but it also has a job to do. The culture of visiting is a system for fostering and maintaining advantageous friendships and drawing households into networks of powerful alliances. In such a culture, visiting is both a discretionary pleasure and a social obligation. When there is someone new and socially significant in the neighbourhood then it would be inexplicably rude *not* to visit. In *Pride and Prejudice*, Mr Bennet, sardonically disengaged though he is from conventional social niceties, makes a point of going to visit Mr Bingley when he moves into Netherfield. By the same token, there will always be those who are *not* visitable. One of the **risks** of Harriet Smith's possible marriage to Robert Martin is that Emma Woodhouse 'could not have visited Mrs Robert Martin, of Abbey-Mill Farm' (*E*: 56). Harriet would have ceased to exist, in Emma's **eyes**, if she had married someone outside of Highbury's social elite. Beyond the inner circle of visitable **friends** and family, in any Austen novel, there is a wider community of the unvisitable. *Persuasion* focuses in redemptive ways on one member of that community, Mrs Smith, whom Anne Elliot insists on visiting despite her father's belief that the impoverished widow is beyond the pale. In a sharply exclusive social world, even members of your own family can fail to make the cut. It's easy to forget, in all the euphoria of its finale, that the end of *Pride and Prejudice* is also a clinically specific roll-call of those who are and aren't welcome at Pemberley. Miss Bingley eagerly retains the 'right of visiting' (*PP*: 430) and so too do Lady Catherine, Mr Bennet, and Mr and Mrs Gardiner. Not welcome at the Darcys' home are Wickham, Mrs Bennet and the Phillipses of Meryton. There may be something refreshingly democratic about Darcy's relationship with the comparatively **poor** Elizabeth, but the lines between the visitable and the unvisitable are as sharply drawn as ever.

Visiting in Austen is always an ambiguous privilege. On the one hand, the opportunity to be a visitor is not something to be lightly turned down. Who wouldn't want to enjoy generously sustained hospitality in grand social settings at other people's expense? Nor can the opportunities for droll people-watching in such contexts be underestimated. The visitor can feature in Austen as a kind of itinerant satirist, a fly-on-the wall observer who peers with disinterested and amused curiosity into a quirky social world, as Charlotte Heywood does when she beholds the rogues' gallery of eccentrics and hypochondriacs on display in Sanditon. But it's not always easy for visitors to carry themselves with such quietly amused self-possession. When Austen's heroines go visiting, it's often without a secure sense of home as a fallback position or permanent emotional headquarters. Catherine Morland and Fanny Price are both launched into society from overcrowded, financially precarious homes. A career in visiting can be associated with feelings of lostness, temporariness and rootlessness. As the Austen heroine moves from one invitation to the next, whether it's a brief stopover or a months-long sojourn, she becomes the drifting citizen of a privileged limbo between the old security of the parental home and the uncertain prospect of some future marital home. In *Persuasion*, when Kellynch Hall is leased to the Crofts, Anne Elliot becomes a serial visitor who has to adapt herself to the habits, customs and preoccupations of 'every little social commonwealth' (*P*: 46) that she passes through. The Austen heroine is often confined by stifling domestic spaces but she needs all the savoir faire of a seasoned traveller. In *Mansfield Park*, when Fanny Price is sent back to Portsmouth on Sir Thomas's instructions, it's hard to say whether this counts as a visit, a homecoming or a period of exile for the novel's subtly displaced heroine. A notably extreme version of the precarity of visitors in Austen is experienced by Catherine Morland, who discovers at Northanger Abbey that the guest who is tolerated one day might be turfed out the next.

Hosts in Austen want visitors – but they also want something *from* their visitors. In ways that may not be immediately obvious to a novice in the field such as Catherine Morland, visiting is a transactional relationship, one in which there can be winners and losers. In *Sense and Sensibility*, the Dashwood sisters receive many opportunities to dine and socialize at Barton Park, ones that they 'pay' for when their private lives become a diverting sideshow for Sir John Middleton and his circle. The dividing line between hospitality and exploitation is often hard to make out. Nor do Austen's hosts always enjoy the upper hand in such dynamics. In *Pride and Prejudice*, Mr Collins invites himself round to Longbourn with a view to making one of the Bennet sisters his wife, but comes away empty-handed. However, when Mr Collins makes himself at home with the Bennets, he is staking out what will literally become his territory when the head of the household dies. The Bennets' cluelessly self-important visitor is also a sinister memento mori.

Visiting can be exhausting. In return for the hospitality she receives, the Austen heroine makes substantial and ongoing contributions to the cultural economy of the home where she stays. She will be kindly looked after but also knowingly appraised, showcased, gossiped about. She will be a decorative addition to the place but she also sometimes has to look after the **children**. The country houses that dominate Austen's social landscapes are not jailhouses, but they have some of a prison's ability to drain and demoralize. When the opportunity arises to visit Pemberley, Elizabeth professes to be 'tired of great houses' (*PP*: 267). She has her own reasons for not wanting to spend time at Darcy's home, but she's not wrong to suggest that a great house can sap your energy. An introductory walkabout can turn into a seemingly endless ordeal. As General Tilney conducts Catherine Morland on a punishingly thorough guided tour of Northanger Abbey, it is not long before she is 'heartily weary of seeing and wondering' (*NA*: 183). Nor is she the only visitor in Austen who has to put in a gruelling shift of visual and cognitive labour on someone else's property. At Hunsford, Mr Collins wants to show his guests 'every article of furniture [...] every walk and cross walk [...] every view [...] the fields in every direction' (*PP*: 177). The young people of *Mansfield Park* undergo something similar at the hands of Mrs Rushworth, who seems ready to expose her visitors to every square inch of Sotherton Court before one of them spots an open door and they spill out into 'air and liberty' (*MP*: 105).

From Northanger Abbey to Southerton Court, the great houses in Austen's fiction seem to feed on the energy and attention of their guests; it is as though they can't exist without a steady stream of visitors to admire their magnificence. At the same time, the owners of great homes can react with a certain proprietorial defensiveness to the people who file so admiringly through their galleries, drawing-rooms and gardens. Visitors are welcome so long as they experience a version of the house that has been officially sanctioned by the owner. The figure of the wayward visitor, one who has their own unofficial or nonstandard experience of the great house, is a troubling presence in Austen's narratives of imposingly grand domesticity. With their insistence on making guests acquainted with absolutely every corner of their property, Austen's tour guides often endeavour to nullify, in advance, the possibility that newcomers will have their own affective relationships with the spaces they have come to occupy. Such controlling behaviour can backfire. In *Northanger Abbey*, for example, it is as though General Tilney's gruelling guided tour makes Catherine Morland all the more determined to discover corners of the Abbey that haven't yet been singled out for attention by her overbearing host.

Given her emphasis on bad hosts and oppressive households, it's no surprise that subversive and resistant visitors also occupy a special place in Austen's imagination. Visiting heroines in her work take some slightly chancy short-cuts into upmarket social environments. In *Northanger Abbey*, when Catherine makes a breathless and unannounced entrance into the Tilneys' house on Milsom Street, she effectively gatecrashes her way into a new social world. When **Jane** Bennet's time as a dinner party guest at Netherfield is prolonged by **illness** into a stay of several days, her visit both signals and enhances the possibility of her becoming a more permanent part of the household. Another visitor, Elizabeth Bennet, is soon with them. The manner of Elizabeth's arrival, with her petticoat 'six inches deep in mud' (*PP*: 39), confirms Louisa and Caroline Bingley in their low opinion of their latest visitor. Elizabeth is greeted as an upstart intruder, a social contaminant in the pristine space of their elegant country house. A visitor even more alarming than Elizabeth Bennet is the heroine of *Lady Susan*, who blazes a trail through various respectable households, a walking, talking antidote to all the impossibly virtuous female visitors of Georgian fiction. With a heroine who tests the limits of hospitality and goodwill wherever she goes, Austen's epistolary novella gleefully inverts the notion of the female visitor as demure wallflower.

In her capacity as Austen's most outrageously aggressive and imposing visitor, Lady Susan's conduct visibly raises a question that her fiction always implies: when does visiting end? Such a question can be asked in respect of individual acts of visiting. Catherine Morland is anxious not to out-stay her welcome at Northanger Abbey, for example, whereas Lady Susan has no scruples about imposing herself indefinitely on her reluctant hosts at Churchill. A longer-term version of the question would be: when, for Austen's heroines, do the visiting years end? As we have seen, the real strategic endgame in the culture of visiting is marriage. The point at which the heroine gets married is the point she can be defined as a grandly secure visitee rather than a perpetually mobile, displaced, precarious visitor. None of which, of course, represents an interruption to the exhausting process of visiting itself, a form of cultural labour that never ends. The visiting will continue but Austen's heroines can at least look forward to the moment when it will be other people doing the seeing and the wondering.

W IS FOR WEST INDIES

In October 1798, Austen and her parents, en route from her brother Edward's home in Kent to the family home in Hampshire, were staying at an inn in Dartford when her personal effects – including her writing-box – were by some **accident** put in a chaise and 'driven away towards Gravesend in their way to the West Indies' (*L*: 15). Luckily, Austen and her misdirected possessions were soon re-united. But why does she mention the West Indies, of all places, when she is imagining a possible final destination for her lost things? The West Indies, an island system in the Caribbean, has since the sixteenth century been perceived from Europe as the scene of conquest, a site of warfare, a hub of power, a source of wealth and a centre of the slave trade. Not that any of this seems to be at the forefront of Austen's mind as she writes to Cassandra. In the context of her humorous aside, the West Indies are roughly synonymous with 'the ends of the earth' or 'the back of beyond' – a region unimaginably and unreachably distant from the world she knows. The journey of Austen's writing-box to this region was only ever a whimsical thought experiment. But what if we take it seriously? What advantages might there be in imaginatively re-locating Jane Austen and her writing to the Caribbean?

It's not as hard as it might seem to relocate Jane Austen to the West Indies because in some notable respects her family were already there. Her father, the Reverend George Austen, was one of the two co-trustees of a sugar plantation on Antigua owned by his **friend** and sometime Oxford contemporary James-Langford Nibbs (1738–95). Cassandra Austen's fiancé, Tom Fowle (1765–97), accompanied his relative Lord Craven to the West Indies in his capacity as private chaplain, and died of yellow fever in San Domingo. Jane's brother Frank Austen commanded HMS Canopus to Antigua in 1805 and fought in a famous naval victory off San Domingo in 1806. When her brother James married Anne Mathew (1759–95), he married into a family with extensive links to the Caribbean. His father-in-law, General Edward Mathew (1728–1805), was born in Antigua and *his* father and grandfather had both held senior positions in the colonial administration in the Leeward Islands. Even leaving aside the web of biographical connections, the West Indies are referenced repeatedly in Austen's fiction. Most famously – and controversially – Sir Thomas Bertram and his son Tom spend an extended period in Antigua, where the master of Mansfield Park owns an estate, presumably a sugar plantation. Significant naval characters in Austen have West Indian connections. William Price's naval career takes him to the Caribbean in *Mansfield Park*, as does Captain Wentworth's in *Persuasion*. Also in *Persuasion*, Mrs Smith's sorry financial predicament is bound up with an unresolved legal dispute about property in the West Indies. In *Sanditon*, meanwhile, the West Indian heiress Miss Lambe is the only person of colour in Austen's fiction. We shouldn't, of course, over-state the extent to which Austen brings the West Indies to life on the page. Her fiction doesn't contain a single scene that is set on West Indian soil. But the unignorable presence in her work of the West Indies as an off-stage scene of adventure, site of business and source of wealth has provoked some of the most vigorous debates in modern Austen scholarship.

Persuasion provides a compact illustration of the shifting roles and positions of the West Indies in Austen's imagination. Wentworth's first romantic interlude with Anne Elliot is framed by periods of active service in the Caribbean. He has been made a commander in the Royal Navy 'in consequence of the action off St. Domingo' (*P*: 28) – we can imagine him fighting alongside Frank Austen – but his role in this victory is not enough to convince Anne's family that he is a safe prospect as a husband. Not long after the engagement is broken off he is 'sent off to the West Indies' (*P*: 70) in command of the *Asp*, the latest chapter in what will be an increasingly illustrious naval career. The West Indies thus seems to have a double role in *Persuasion*. It is a testing-ground for heroic advancement, a place where Wentworth can disprove those who doubted his prospects as a sailor. But it is also a place of exile from the provincial England of *Persuasion*, one that places Wentworth at a seemingly irretrievable distance from Anne.

The denouement of *Persuasion* involves a shift in the way it thinks about the Caribbean. Mrs Smith escapes from poverty when, aided by Wentworth, she recovers some property of her late husband's in the West Indies. The West Indies continue to exert a certain pull on Austen's imagination, albeit now in economic, financial and legal terms. They are no longer poignantly and exotically unreachable, nor are they idealized as a scene of stirring military success; rather, they feature as a solution to an economic problem, a previously unlooked-for source of freedom from financial anxieties. As the sheltered widow of **Bath** becomes someone with a lucrative stake in the West Indies, the region is not a **theatre** of war but a place of business.

In *Persuasion*, all we know about the location of Mrs Smith's holdings is that they are *somewhere* in the West Indies. *Mansfield Park* is altogether more specific in pinpointing Antigua as the location of a key (if never directly represented) storyline. One of the Leeward Islands, 'discovered' during Columbus' second voyage to the new world, Antigua would be formally colonized in the seventeenth century, becoming part of what was known as the British West Indies. It was, Brian Dyde (2000) explains in a compact history of the island, a strategically advantageous location, one that became the Royal Navy's base in the east Caribbean where the fleet sought to protect shipping lanes and safeguard British interests in the region. British rule would be continuous through to the late twentieth century but the threat of invasion flared up periodically, not least during the revolutionary wars of the late eighteenth and early nineteenth centuries. Sugar was the key crop, and enslaved African men and women were brought to the island in their thousands by the Royal African Company to work on the plantations. Antigua never saw uprisings on the scale of those in Jamaica or Haiti, but the possibility of slave rebellion would be in the air until its abolition in 1834 and the 'problem' of runaway slaves was an ongoing source of concern for politicians and plantation owners.

All of this, on the face of it, is a long way off from a country house in Northamptonshire. Indeed, on a cursory reading Antigua might seem to be little more than a place-name in *Mansfield Park*. What matters about Sir Thomas's voyage is not the fact that it is to Antigua but that it is away from home. His business affairs in the West Indies get him out of the way so that we can inspect the gap he leaves in a social world that he ordinarily dominates and defines. With Sir Thomas away, and with Lady Bertram drifting in and out of consciousness on the sofa, Mansfield Park's usual standards of vetting and quality control are temporarily suspended, and what is ordinarily a solemn mansion becomes a veritable funhouse thronged by revellers and pleasure seekers. It doesn't seem to matter that Sir Thomas is in Antigua when all of this is going on; what matters is that he is elsewhere.

The West Indian island does however occupy a crucial position in the symbolic geography of the novel. Mansfield Park, under the temporary control of the **young** Bertrams and their friends, is a space of play, high-spirits and self-indulgence. The Antigua to which Sir Thomas voyages is a space of work, business and arduous responsibility – not to mention the possibility of moral rehabilitation for his dissolute son Tom, who accompanies him to the Caribbean. On Sir Thomas's mental map of the Atlantic, Antigua is not just a source of wealth but an offshore reformatory where a good-for-nothing young European can get a chance at redemption. It's no coincidence in this context that Antigua literally means *old* or *ancient* – the legend goes that it was named as such by Christopher Columbus in 1493, in honour of an iconic mural, *La Virgen de la Antigua*, in the Catedral de Santa María de la Sede in Seville (Dyde 2000: 9–11). Sir Thomas's relocation to Antigua is the first move in a complex intergenerational conflict between old and young, between traditional values and the feckless modernity of the young delinquents in Mansfield Park.

Despite its crucial position in *Mansfield Park*'s imaginative geography, Antigua – its people, its social spaces, its landscapes – is never seen in the novel. Sir Thomas's **letters** home paint an entirely abstract picture of 'business' (*MP*: 125) and 'anxiety' (*MP*: 125), of 'Unfavourable circumstances' and 'very great uncertainty' (*MP*: 43). Insofar as Antigua is perceived in these letters it is done so as a series of unspecified workplace problems. The closest we get to an on-the-ground feel for the place is via its effects on Sir Thomas's body. On his return he has 'grown thinner and had the burnt, fagged, worn look of fatigue and a hot climate' (*MP*: 208–9). Sir Thomas's emaciated, sunburnt and worn-out frame is the only visual souvenir of Antigua in this novel. His body tells one story, but not all his memories of the place are harrowing ones. In the company of Henry Crawford and William Price, for example, he expansively recalls the 'balls of Antigua' (*MP*: 292). The notion that Antigua might have been the scene of *pleasure* for Sir Thomas is tantalizingly underdeveloped. Were there times when he enjoyed being there as much as his family enjoyed being rid of him?

The decisive position of Antigua in *Mansfield Park* has been highlighted in an influential postcolonial reading of the novel by Edward Said (1994). According to Said, no account of the civilized splendour of the Bertrams' Northamptonshire estate can omit to mention its dependence on wealth that flows from the West Indies. 'The Bertrams,' he writes, 'could not have been possible without the slave trade' (1994: 112). Numerous modern critics have wrestled with the issues of colonialism and slavery as they are raised in (or veiled by) Austen's fiction (see Ferguson 1991; Wiltshire 2003; Boulukos 2006; Looser 2021). A particular crux in *Mansfield Park* is the moment when Fanny Price regrets that her attempt to broach the subject of the slave trade in conversation with her uncle and cousins is greeted with 'such a dead silence!' (*MP*: 231). How are we to interpret this silence? Whatever it may signify – shame? anger? incuriosity? indifference? – the subject of slavery seems to be non-starter with at least some members of the Bertram household. Whether Austen's own fiction is itself culpably reticent on the horrors of slavery is a moot point. The fact that slavery is even broached here as a potential talking point suggests that it is by no means taboo in Austen's imagination. The silence around slavery is broken in other ways too. It has been suggested, for example, that Fanny Price – downtrodden, exploited and overworked – is a kind of 'slave' in the Bertram household. Not that this is a particularly tasteful or illuminating analogy. There are all sorts of very obvious problems in conflating the experience of enslaved people in the Caribbean with that of a white European woman who, by comparison, leads an extraordinarily privileged life (Ferguson 1991). More subtle is a possible allusion in the novel's title. Some contemporary readers of *Mansfield Park* may have associated its title with Lord Mansfield, the Lord Chief Justice of the English court from 1756 to 1788, who in the case of *Somerset v Stewart* (1772) famously ruled that slavery had no basis in English common law. Despite the silence that greets Fanny when she broaches the subject, *Mansfield Park* is evidently in search of ways to talk about slavery.

Though they engage in subtly revealing ways with the region, *Mansfield Park* and *Persuasion* represent a West Indies without West Indians. *Sanditon*, Austen's final, unfinished novel, is different. Its cast of characters includes one Miss Lambe, a 'young West Indian of large fortune, in delicate health' (*LM*: 200). Miss Lambe is 'half mulatto' (*LM*: 202) and for this reason we can surmise that she may be the grand-daughter of a slave-owner. All the indications are that Miss Lambe would have been a significant character in this text, but up to the point at which Austen abandoned her work on the novel, the West Indian heiress is evoked largely through rumour and speculative gossip among the residents of Sanditon, some of which is confirmed by the narrator. The primary reportable fact about Miss Lambe that gains traction in the neighbourhood gossip is not her ethnicity but her money. As Sara Salih (2006) notes, no one in the novel makes a fuss about the presence of a person of colour at Sanditon, but there is a lot of talk about the fact that she is rich. 'No people spend more freely, I believe, than West Indians' (*LM*: 170), says Mr Parker, in the context of a debate about whether a nouveaux riche big spender might have an inflationary impact on the local economy.

Other kinds of inflation are associated with Miss Lambe's arrival in Sanditon. Her impending **visit** is trailed not just by speculation about her wealth but by a revealing case of mistaken identity. Sanditon is a health resort that is eager to drum up business, and when word gets around that

X IS FOR XIS

In the first week of the final year of her life, Austen wrote a short **letter** to her eight-year-old niece, Cassy Austen. 'Ym raed Yssac', it begins, 'I hsiw uoy a yppah wen raey. Ruoy xis snisuoc emac ereh yadretsey, dna dah hcae a eceip fo ekac' (L: 338), and continues in the same cryptic vein for several sentences. The process of decoding it is only mildly taxing: once we start reading backwards, the letter soon yields up its secrets – *xis* is readable as 'six', and so forth. But it is not simply a question of reading backwards. While the letters in individual words appear back-to-front, the individual words appear in the correct order. So we can't just reverse the direction of readerly travel as we scan the text; rather, we need to read this letter forwards and backwards at the same time (though whichever way you read the *I* that signifies Austen is the same). The letter thus makes us work a little harder than we ordinarily would to obtain what turns out to be some rather humdrum family news. Frank has begun learning Latin. Sally Benham has a new green gown. They feed the robin every day. There is nothing tremendously compelling here, no delicate secrets or explosive revelations encoded within those tantalizingly cryptic sentences. Indeed, we wouldn't linger on the contents of this letter at all if its style hadn't obliged us to make something of an effort to decode them. Our reward for this effort is not the information itself but the pleasure of negotiating a cryptic linguistic **obstacle** and joining Austen and her niece in a private linguistic world, one from which less perspicacious readers – those whom the author famously refers to as 'dull Elves' (L: 210) – are excluded.

Austen's new year letter to Cassy is a likeable instance of what we can call her cryptophilia, her delight in word-games, secrets and riddles, her love of the hidden and the non-obvious. It is a letter that experiments with language, makes demands on its reader and creates pleasure from its own riddling complexity. The letter also performs a minor feat of linguistic alchemy, transforming humdrum news items into a pleasing literary construct. We could say that two Austens are visible in this letter. One is a *realist* Austen, a writer whose primary loyalty is to the unremarkable, the ordinary and humble, and who wants to rescue the overlooked quotidiana of everyday life – the bits of family news that hardly even qualify as narrative – from obscurity or oblivion. The other is a *ludic* Austen, a purveyor of ingenious word games and formal tricks whose writing proudly flaunts its playful, inventive, riddling and self-reflexive qualities even at the **risk** of alienating 'dull' readers. It is not immediately obvious that these two Austens are compatible. One is a writer who places her words at the service of an external reality that she tries to capture in all its humble ordinariness. The other is an author whose writing is in some sense self-serving – a tricksy, self-conscious practice whose stylistic ingenuity threatens to eclipse its unassuming subject matter. Even as we crack the code of this letter to Cassy we may continue to puzzle over the more taxing conundrum of Austen's dual literary identity.

Austen's fascination with games and play is by no means restricted to her letters. Her novels abound in games, riddles, conundrums and other diversions. When Austen's characters are not going to plays or staging plays of their own, they enjoy a range of recreational pursuits from card games and word puzzles to backgammon and billiards. A significant hallmark of a society of leisure, these games and pastimes give structure and purpose to a social world that is not governed by the imperatives of labour. Games have their own rules, and create their own provisional realities, but the world of games in Austen is never wholly insulated from the world of lived experience. In their structured, rule-bound, systematic qualities, games are like art. To the extent that they stir emotion and involve **risk** and unpredictability, games are like life.

Nowhere are the ludic qualities of Austen's realist writing more conspicuous than in her most exuberantly playful novel, *Emma*. From the early craze for elaborate riddles among Emma's social circle to the conundrums and witticisms that go down so badly during the ill-tempered expedition to Box Hill, *Emma* is a novel of puzzles that itself plays an elaborate game with the reader, withholding as it does the key fact that **Jane** Fairfax is secretly engaged to Frank Churchill. Even though clues to Frank's relationship with Jane have been artfully sprinkled through the preceding narrative, such clues only become legible when we re-trace our steps through the text. When we become privy to its secrets, and begin to revise our understanding of the narrative, we will realize that *Emma* obliges us to do what Cassy Austen has to do – we need to read this text forwards and backwards at the same time.

As we begin to appreciate the elaborate game that *Emma* has played with our readerly awareness, we might be moved to quote some words of Mr Elton's: 'what reverse we have!' (*E*: 76). These words are taken from

Elton's riddle on courtship, which he delivers to an audience that includes Emma and Harriet Smith. Emma solves this particular riddle easily enough but she misses what will in retrospect seem obvious – the answer to the riddle is 'courtship', but the riddle as delivered at Hartfield is itself an *act* of courtship, one that is implicitly directed at Austen's heroine. Emma understands the riddle's internal content, that is to say, but not its emotional trajectory, perhaps because she is insufficiently vain to imagine that people will fall in love with her – or perhaps because she is insufficiently attentive to the behavioural clues that might reveal such feelings. Elton, as Emma will in time acknowledge, is the 'reverse' of everything she had thought him to be. We can shake our heads over Emma's misreading of Elton, but any sense of cognitive superiority we may enjoy over her is neatly deflated when we discover ('What reverse we have!') that *Emma* is itself a large-scale riddle that we have been misreading all along.

Linguistic games such as Mr Elton's cryptic poem often hinge on a 'reverse', a moment of cognitive turnaround that obliges and enables us to see things differently. And such local moments of revelation-through-play, as we have seen in the case of *Emma*, provide an image in miniature of the overall architecture of a novel that is constructed around an eye-opening reversal of expectations. Games-playing in Austen is not merely a diverting hobby, then, but a form of training in the salutary cognitive activity of reading backwards and forwards at the same time. To read *xis* as *six* is to engage flexibly with narrative sequences and the secrets and surprises they may harbour. To read *xis* as *six* is also to turn an ending into a beginning – or, rather, to convert a linear verbal structure into something more like a narrative spiral. Once again, this back-to-front word game can provide us with a neat microcosm of Austen's novelistic methods. Austen's tendency to send our attention in two directions at once has been remarked by John Wiltshire, who notices how *Pride and Prejudice* explores its characters' – and by extension its readers' – partial, conflicting and continually revised memories and misrememberings of significant details in the novel (2014: 51–71). Making sense of things, in this text, involves a continual revisiting of words, gestures and expressions – a smile, a stray remark – whose full meaning may not have been available first time round. Do Elizabeth's recollections of her first impressions of Darcy and Wickham square with what she does and says at the time? We can check, if we want – not simply to uncover inconsistencies in her version of events but rather to explore critically but sympathetically the complexity of memory as it is represented and experienced through this text.

These spiralling and recessive qualities in Austen might also help us re-think one of the more problematic qualities of her novels: their endings. Endings, as Austen manages them, can be curiously unsatisfactory. The conclusion of *Northanger Abbey* risks breaking the spell by alerting us to the 'tell-tale compression of the pages' (*NA*: 259) of the book in our hands, while the final chapter of *Mansfield Park*, a novel whose storyline has entered some seriously dark territory, exhorts 'other pens' to 'dwell on guilt and misery' (*MP*: 533) as it pivots breezily towards its happy ending. In both cases it is hard not to feel that the ending, in its prematurity and artificiality, is a betrayal of the complex, unresolved story that led up to it. Perhaps, however, these endings might be read as tongue-in-check concessions to the fact that even though human experience is ongoing, any narrative that purports to capture that ongoingness will 'fail' because it can't not end. These are not the endings that we want, or that will satisfy us, but Austen knows that, and she knows that they may well send us indignantly back to everything that has gone before in all its unresolved complexity. The ending of an Austen novel, in other words, is not a botched climax but an artful counter-climax that functions as a stimulus to re-reading. And Austen has of course already made back-tracking and re-reading part of our first-time experience of her fiction. We are already re-reading her novels long before we get to the 'end' that never arrives.

Y IS FOR YOUNG

It seems almost too obvious to say that when Austen writes, she writes about youth – about young people, that is to say, rather than **children**. Her novels are largely indifferent to the infancy of their heroines. Fanny Price in *Mansfield Park* gets a couple of chapters devoted to her childhood; Elizabeth Bennet in *Pride and Prejudice* gets nothing at all. All the emphasis in Austen is on the moment when a young protagonist is launched from the family home into a complex social world where the thrills of autonomy and mobility contend with new anxieties about marriage, money, property and status. From *Northanger Abbey* to *Sanditon*, her fiction depicts young people in the process of discovering themselves as they are discovered by society at large. One discovery that youth has to come to terms with is the fact of its own temporariness. In *The Watsons*, Elizabeth says to her sister Emma that she would be happy to be single 'if one could be young for ever' (*LM*: 82). Socializing, flirtation and courtship in Austen are exhilarating precisely because they take place against the background of a relentless countdown towards the 'years of danger' (*P*: 7). *Persuasion*, the most suspenseful thing she ever wrote, is the story of a heroine who *seems* to have crossed the threshold from youth into age – or, rather, into the post-youth state of aunthood – before she seizes an eleventh-hour opportunity to make the same journey in the opposite direction.

What exactly counts as young in Austen's world? A revealing answer to this question is implicitly offered by Captain Wentworth in *Persuasion*. Talking expansively about his desire to get married, he announces that 'Any body between fifteen and thirty may have me for asking' (*P*: 66). Austen evidently concurs with Wentworth's definition of the window of marriageability in a young woman's life. Her fiction focuses mainly on heroines in their late teens (Catherine Morland, Elinor and Marianne Dashwood, Fanny Price) and early twenties (Elizabeth Bennet, Emma Woodhouse). At the unthinkably advanced age of twenty-seven, Anne Elliot in *Persuasion* is a limit case, though that novel's story flows from, and intently focuses on, the consequences of a decision its protagonist makes as a nineteen-year-old. A different rule of marriageability seems to apply to men in Austen. The romantic male leads in her fiction are in their twenties (Henry Tilney, Edward Ferrars, Darcy, Edmund Bertram, Frank Churchill, Captain Wentworth) or thirties (Colonel Brandon, Mr Knightley). One privilege enjoyed by men in her world is a less pressurized relationship with time. As they approach their fourth decade, her male characters have no special reason to think that they are approaching the years of danger.

'Young', in the language of Austen's fiction, is tantalizingly synonymous with 'single'; it is an epithet that marks someone out as at the very least a *thinkable* prospect in romantic or matrimonial terms. If someone in Austen is referred to as an 'amiable youth' (*NA*: 9), then we can take it that they are eligible, attractive and unattached. And if Austen gives us precise information about someone's age, then you can often expect that person to get married or at least to be active on the marriage market. She is always, as John Mullan puts it, an 'age-sensitive' (2012: 13) novelist, although her interest in the specifics of people's ages fades once they are married – or once they are no longer deemed to be marriageable. In *Emma*, for example, we know that Harriet Smith is seventeen, Emma Woodhouse is twenty, Frank Churchill is twenty-three, Robert Martin is twenty-four, Mr Elton is twenty-six or twenty-seven and Mr Knightley is 'about seven or eight-and-thirty' (*E*: 8). Information about these characters' ages circulates in *Emma* like a price-list for commodities on the Highbury marriage market. Readers who would like to know the ages of Mr Woodhouse, Mrs Bates or Miss Bates will have to make their best guess.

A character's 'youth', in Austen, is frequently understood not just in terms of their marital status but via perceptions of their attitude and behaviour. When Anne Elliot mulls over the maudlin widower Captain Benwick, she reflects that 'He is younger than I am; younger in feeling, if not in fact; younger as a man' (*P*: 105). Youth, in other words, is not simply a matter of countable years. Feelings count too – including the feelings of others. No one in Austen gets more exercised about another character's 'youth' than Knightley does about Frank Churchill's in *Emma*. Frank, who will turn out to be a mischievous, revitalizing presence in the creaking gerontocracy of Highbury, makes himself unpopular with Knightley simply by virtue of existing as a young, unattached, eligible man. At issue, before Mr Weston's son has even arrived in Highbury is the question of whether Frank, at twenty-three, counts as 'young' (*E*: 103) – and whether a 'young man' (*E*: 132) should be able to command his own time. The back-and-forth about this last question is a surprisingly detailed one, given that

Emma and her circle have not yet met the young man in question. 'Young' Frank is controversial because 'young' here is a code for a tantalizing sense of eligibility that radiates from Frank even before he makes his presence felt in the novel.

Knightley is eager for Frank's youth to count against him. 'Your amiable young man', he declares to Emma, 'is a very weak young man' (*E*: 159); towards the end of the novel he is still insistently describing Frank as a 'very, very young man' (*E*: 486). The fact that Frank is twenty-three is something he never retires of repeating (*E*: 157, 161, 466), each time with some mixture of indignation, disbelief or scorn. It's no mystery why Knightley allows himself to be so elaborately vexed by Frank's youth. You don't have to be a Mrs Bennet to foresee that the arrival of an eligible, unattached young man in Highbury may pique Emma's interest. Knightley's objections to Frank's youth are, however, revealingly contradictory. On the one hand, he wants to paint Frank as a juvenile upstart who has no business making himself a fetching new catalyst of Highbury sociability. On the other, he claims that Frank is more than old enough to take control of his personal affairs, stand up to his manipulative bully of an aunt and pay proper attention and respect to his father and stepmother at Highbury. It is as though Knightley will use any argument, however contradictory, to persuade his audience – and himself – that simply being twenty-three years old is an unforgivable solecism on Frank's part.

Subtly at issue throughout *Emma* is the way Frank's exuberant impact on Highbury prompts Knightley to reconsider his own studied non-youthfulness. When Frank arrives in Highbury, it's not long before the dancing breaks out, and Knightley is obviously reluctant to throw himself into sociability that has been orchestrated by his young rival. When Knightley attends the ball at the Crown, it is a source of regret to Austen's heroine that he chooses not to **dance** and prefers to join the 'husbands, and fathers, and whist-players' on the sidelines, 'so young as he looked!' (*E*: 352). In Emma's **eyes**, Knightley's stiff, stand-offish behaviour places himself on the wrong side of a division between lively young dancers and fuddy-duddy spectators. What gets Knightley dancing, curiously enough, is the sight of another man who is a bit too eager to embrace sedentary maturity. When it is suggested that Mr Elton might dance with Harriet Smith, the twenty-seven-year-old vicar, in a cruel moment of faux self-deprecation, declares that he is an 'old married man' (*E*: 354) whose dancing days are over. Knightley, given an opportunity to rejuvenate himself in Emma's eyes, steps in and leads Harriet to the dancefloor. Whether he consciously acknowledges it or not,

Knightley ultimately has his twenty-three-year-old bête noire to thank for this opportunity to perform to such advantage in front of Emma.

Knightley's amusingly and revealingly vexed relationship with Frank Churchill is one manifestation of a question that is raised continually in Austen: what does society see in, and want from, the young? When the young are perceived as a collective in her fiction they are often perceived as a problem. Some of her characters need little prompting to moralize about the young – even if they indict their former selves in the process. When Mrs Smith in *Persuasion* recalls the disreputable circles in which she once moved, she declares that: 'I was very young, and associated only with the young and we were a thoughtless, gay set, without any strict rules of conduct' (*P*: 218). But the buoyant collective gaiety of the young is not always quite so easy to dismiss. Consider *Mansfield Park*, where the high-spirited antics of the young people who gather in Sir Thomas's absence amount to a rowdy juvenile takeover of a grandly solemn country house. Austen's representations of youthful pleasure-seeking in this novel are never less than ambivalent. She can't seem to decide whether to tut-tut with high-minded disapproval at what young people get up to when they are left to their own devices or to let herself be swept along by all the giddy excitement. What the narrator of *Emma* refers to as the 'tyrannic influence of youth on youth' (*E*: 15), and what would now be called peer pressure, powerfully energizes the youth-centred chapters of *Mansfield Park*. Austen's fiction needs the energy of a 'thoughtless, gay set', however much it might seem to side with Sir Thomas in his draconian crackdown on the youth culture that has colonized the Bertram household.

The master of Mansfield Park expects obedience, propriety and decorum from the young; he wants to see reflected in them a flattering mirror of his own personal dignity. But Sir Thomas's authoritarianism is not the only prism through which the younger generation are perceived in Austen. There are other eminent characters in her work who, when they look to the young, do so in search of narrative pleasure. In *Sense and Sensibility*, for example, the faintly vampire-like Sir John Middleton delights in 'collecting about him more young people than his house would hold' (*SS*: 39). Young people are brought into his sphere of influence as an on-call narrative resource, a fund of gossip and amusement for those who have nothing to do but derive vicarious entertainment from the antics of their youthful guests. Only a steady throughput of young people at Barton Park will meet Sir John's need for titillating reports of secret attachments, romantic indiscretions and mystery beaux.

It often seems as though young people in Austen are at the mercy of the older generation's contradictory desires. On the one hand, the young should be decently and properly undesiring. The risqué theatrics at Mansfield Park are cancelled by Sir Thomas. It is unthinkable for Mr Woodhouse that Emma will ever get married. On the other hand, matchmakers and gossips from Mrs Bennet to Sir John Middleton exhibit an unseemly desire to witness, shape and narrate the desires of the young. Youthful desire is subject to powerful taboos even as it is expected to make itself divertingly visible for an older audience. As Austen's young protagonists begin to negotiate these contradictory demands, the years of danger have already begun.

Z IS FOR ZIGZAG

When Emma Woodhouse flatly rejects Mr Elton's **unexpected** proposal of marriage, the scene has been set for what promises to be a scene of exquisite awkwardness. A confined carriage en route from Randalls to Highbury has provided a scene of intimacy that Elton wants to prolong and formalize, and that Emma can't wait to escape. But it turns out that their tête-a-tête is not quite so painfully cringe-making as you might expect. '[T]heir straightforward emotions', we are informed, 'left no room for the little zigzags of embarrassment' (*E*: 143). Sheer exasperated annoyance, for both parties, overrides any of the squirming self-consciousness that our heroine and her would-be husband might otherwise be feeling in the circumstances.

Elsewhere in Austen, however, there is plenty of room for embarrassment and its little zigzags. Encompassed in her narratives of embarrassment are everything from fleeting moments of self-consciousness to the kind of humiliatingly sustained misreadings and misjudgements by which Catherine Morland and Emma Woodhouse are put to intense shame. Austen's fiction is sympathetic always to the predicament of those who are plunged into the ordeal of embarrassment (or 'confusion' or 'consciousness' – the terms are roughly interchangeable), alive to the painful comic possibilities of such experiences, and ready to elicit moral lessons from them. Nor does she overlook the possibility that embarrassment might also be a source of *pleasure* – for the reader and possibly even for the embarrassed person.

Why does Austen use the zigzag, of all possible figures, as a kind of hieroglyphic notation for the experience of embarrassment? On a visual level, a line that abruptly changes direction seems to trace the jerky self-consciousness of **eyes** that don't know where to look, of a gaze that darts around the room, of sightlines broken when two people can't bring themselves to face one another. A zigzag might also be suggestive of a head that twists uncomfortably, or a body that pivots and squirms on its axis as though to deflect unwanted attention, or the unpredictable itinerary of someone who doesn't want to be caught. On the page, a zigzag tells an awkward kind of story. A line that gets jaggedly in its own way might serve as a thumbnail sketch of an Austen storyline as it artfully and effortfully zigs and zags its way past all the **obstacles** – not least the stumbling block of embarrassing people and circumstances – that lie in its path.

Embarrassment makes its victim the protagonist of a small drama of unwanted visibility. In *Sense and Sensibility*, Marianne, in the confusion of embarrassment, is unable to look at Willoughby when they enter her house together after her **accident** (*SS*: 51). Later in the novel, when they meet again in London, it will be Willoughby who can't look Marianne in the eye (*SS*: 201). One of the exquisite discomforts of embarrassment is the way it makes awkwardly conspicuous those who would give anything to vanish into invisibility. The blush, in which the body perversely proclaims that it has something to hide, is a somatic giveaway to which the **young** heroines of Austen's novels are all notably prone. From Catherine Morland to Anne Elliot, they have not 'outlived the age of blushing' (*P*: 52), and their various flushes and reddenings both invite and resist interpretation.

Blushes are conspicuously visible but this does not always mean that they are easy to interpret. Nothing in our repertoire of body language, as Penny Gay remarks, is more definitively untheatrical than the blush (2002: 88). That moment of involuntary reddening, in which characters are ambushed at a physiological level by their own powerful reactions to one another, is not something that can be scripted or premeditated. As Katie Halsey (2006) has shown, however, even if the blushing body appears to be speaking with involuntary candour, it is always possible to misunderstand what it is saying. A blush discloses evidence of an inner life without providing guidance on how to read that evidence. Emma Woodhouse repeatedly misreads embarrassment. She wrongly assumes Harriet Smith's blushes are about Mr Elton (*E*: 55), and she mis-attributes **Jane** Fairfax's 'deep blush of consciousness' (*E*: 262) at the pianoforté to her supposed relationship with Mr Dixon. When Emma confidently predicts that Harriet's relationship with Elton will be an 'an alliance which can never raise a blush in either of us' (*E*: 79) she couldn't be more wrong about what will turn into an embarrassing debacle for all concerned. Austen's heroine is asking for trouble when she makes the avoidance of embarrassment into a principle of social propriety.

Embarrassment is always intimately related to time. It is an experience that we prolong in ardently wanting it to be over, in which we are teased and taunted by past versions of ourselves. Episodes of embarrassment can live in the memory with horrendous clarity and immediacy. Social humiliation can gather its own terrible momentum as when 'one mortification succeeded another' (*NA*: 50) for Catherine Morland in *Northanger Abbey*. In the grip of embarrassment's cruelly self-perpetuating body language, she finds herself 'blushing again that she had blushed before' (*NA*: 210). Like many Austen heroines, she is sent on zigzagging mental journeys back and forward in time. As she squirms retrospectively about the 'grossly injurious suspicions which she must ever blush to have entertained' (*NA*: 206) and lingers over every 'memento of past folly' (*NA*: 206), Catherine becomes the mortified curator of all the evidence of her humiliating misjudgements.

Like Catherine Morland, Emma Woodhouse experiences her recent personal history as a series of unforgettably embarrassing lessons in her own fallibility – lessons that prolong and repeat themselves in insistently uncomfortable ways. As Austen's heroines live through shaming flashbacks, they experience embarrassment as a way of reckoning with that which is over but not over. When Harriet Smith bumps into Robert Martin and his sister at Ford's, she encounters a past that hasn't gone away. Perhaps the most dramatic set-piece of shared embarrassment and unfinished emotional business in Austen is the encounter between Elizabeth Bennet and Darcy at Pemberley, an unexpected rendezvous at which 'the cheeks of each were overspread with the deepest blush' (*PP*: 278). In these supremely awkward encounters, the figure of the ex- or the rejected suitor carries within them the capacity for the past to embarrass the present simply by virtue of continuing to exist.

Implicit in Austen's narratives of embarrassment is the notion that we always have more to learn from the memories that embarrass us than from the ones that flatter us. Sir Walter Elliot will never find anything to mortify him in the Baronetage. References in Austen's fiction to that which cannot be recalled 'without a blush' (*E*: 447) suggest a certain fundamental intimacy between embarrassment and recollection; it is as though the faculty of memory lies not in the mind but in the skin, the face and the blood vessels. Relatedly, there are times in her work when embodied shame seems to be synonymous with thought itself. There is a moment in *Emma*, for example, where the heroine 'blushed to think' (*E*: 146) about her misreading of Mr Elton's matrimonial intentions. 'Blushed to think', in this context, means that Emma *blushed at the thought of* her previous misjudgements. But also legible here is the notion that Emma blushed *in order to think*. The blush, in other words, is not simply a fleeting physical side-effect of a certain thought process but rather the very mechanism through which that process is activated. Thinking and remembering cannot be performed without a blush.

The thoughts provoked by embarrassment tend to be intensely self-centred and painfully autobiographical. In the ordeal of shameful recollection, we viscerally re-experience chapters we'd rather forget from the story of our own lives. There is however an intriguing preoccupation in Austen with embarrassment not as self-consciousness but as *other*-consciousness. What makes the Austen protagonist squirm and cringe is not simply or exclusively their own mortifying behaviour; sometimes, it is the conduct of family and **friends** that exposes them to mortification. *Pride and Prejudice* is, amongst other things, a novel-length exploration of what it means to be embarrassed by your own family. Elizabeth's behaviour is not without its embarrassing moments, but the other Bennets – with the angelic exception of Jane – give her a huge number of extra reasons to squirm. When Lydia Bennet and Wickham get married, they do so with no trace of embarrassment. It is up to Lydia's relatives to feel embarrassed on her behalf. '*She* [Elizabeth] blushed, and Jane blushed; but the cheeks of the two who caused their confusion, suffered no variation of colour' (*PP*: 349). Being embarrassed, in this context, seems to be a mandatory form of emotional labour. Lydia blithely shirks her responsibilities in this area but *someone* has to do it.

Reflecting on the issue of shared mortification, Juliet McMaster has suggested that Austen is a writer who single-handedly makes 'family shame' (1995: 63) a theme for the modern novelist. McMaster writes in this context with particular reference to *The Watsons*, a novel in which a refined young woman squirms in the presence of comparatively vulgar and tactless relatives. It's a pattern that we can recognize in other Austen novels. Elizabeth Bennet spends a lot of *Pride and Prejudice* 'blushing for her mother' (*PP*: 47). In *Mansfield Park*, when Fanny Price is back amid the noise and disorder of the family home in Portsmouth, she feels 'shame for the home in which he [Henry Crawford] found her' (*MP*: 464). In all of these cases, it's impossible not to acknowledge the role of social and class differences in producing embarrassment. Refinement is embarrassed by coarseness, sophistication by vulgarity, elegance by squalor. The figure of the embarrassed person locates themselves on one side of a cultural division but blushes to acknowledge that they belong in significant ways to the other. The experience of family shame in Austen is thus a way of owning what you disown. In the very act of blushing the Austen heroine acknowledges membership of and intimate affinity with everything that she so fastidiously disavows.

It can be tempting to moralize about embarrassment in Austen, to nod sagely as her heroines are shamed into better versions of themselves. But there is another side to the experience of embarrassment in her work, one that is linked to pleasure rather than to improving moral lessons. Austen's novels are of course an inexhaustible source of pleasure for those readers who enjoy what Eve Kosofsky Sedgwick famously calls the spectacle of a 'Girl Being Taught a Lesson' (1991: 833). Embarrassment can be framed as a morally edifying loss of dignity – what is referred to, in *Emma*, as 'profitable humiliation' (*E*: 196). But humiliation, as various readers have noted, is not without its potentially delectable qualities. Ashly Bennett has written on the 'pleasurable dimensions of shame' in Austen (2015: 382) while Mary Ann O'Farrell links embarrassment in the author's work to 'the thrill of being known, the *frisson* of exposure' (1997: 23). For a character with an exhibitionistic streak there might be nothing more powerfully gratifying than what Austen calls, in *Northanger Abbey*, the 'shame of being caught' (*NA*: 169). You might even say that the shame of being caught is the central motivating impulse behind the heroine's nocturnal adventures in that novel: Catherine Morland steals into off-limits areas in the Abbey in order to be found out in the act of finding things out; she sneaks around after dark so as to emerge into a thrillingly intensified form of visibility. Nor is she the only Austen heroine whose embarrassing behaviour might be read as an unconscious exercise in attention-seeking. When Emma Woodhouse says that 'I deserve to be under a continual blush all the rest of my life' (*E*: 367), she seems to be in no mood for her mistakes to be forgiven and forgotten. As she speculates about an appropriate punishment for her blinkered and self-serving behaviour, however, our contrite heroine has conveniently stumbled across a way to give her old narcissistic habits a new lease of life. A perpetual blush might be a small price to pay for a lifetime of attention.

WORKS CITED

Aers, D. (1981), 'Community and Morality: Towards Reading Jane Austen', in
    D. Aers, J. Cook and D. Punter (eds), *Romanticism and Ideology: Studies in
    English Writing 1765–1830*, 118–36, London: Routledge.

Amis, M. (2001), *The War against Cliché: Essays and Reviews 1971–2000*, London:
    Vintage.

Auerbach, N. (1986), *Romantic Imprisonment: Women and Other Glorified Outcasts*,
    New York, NY: Columbia University Press.

Austen-Leigh, J. E. (2002), *'A Memoir of Jane Austen' and Other Family
    Recollections*, ed. K. Sutherland, Oxford: Oxford University Press.

Bennett, A. (2015), 'Shame and Sensibility: Jane Austen's Humiliated Heroines',
    Studies in Romanticism, 54 (3): 377–400.

Boulukos, G. E. (2006), '*Mansfield Park* and the Amelioration of Slavery', *Novel*, 39
    (3): 361–83.

Brownstein, R. M. (1982), *Becoming a Heroine: Reading about Women in Novels*,
    New York, NY: Columbia University Press.

Chwe, M. S. Y. (2013), *Jane Austen, Game Theorist*, Princeton, NJ: Princeton
    University Press.

Clery, E. J. (2017), *Jane Austen: The Banker's Sister*, London: Biteback.

Coley, N. G. (1982), 'Physicians and the Chemical Analysis of Mineral Water in
    Eighteenth Century England', *Medical History*, 26: 123–44.

Craig, S. (2015), *Jane Austen and the State of the Nation*, Basingstoke: Palgrave.

Cunningham, V. (1994), *In the Reading Gaol: Postmodernity, Texts, and History*,
    Oxford: Blackwell.

Davidson, J. (2017), *Reading Jane Austen*, Cambridge: Cambridge University Press.

Davis, G. and P. Bonsall (1996), *Bath: A New History*, Staffordshire: Keele
    University Press.

Deresiewicz, W. (2004), *Jane Austen and the Romantic Poets*, New York, NY:
    Columbia University Press.

Derrida, J. (1992), *Given Time I: Counterfeit Money*, trans. P. Kamuf, Chicago, IL:
    University of Chicago Press.

Doody, M. (2016), *Jane Austen's Names: Riddles, Persons, Places*, Chicago, IL:
    University of Chicago Press.

Dow Adams, T. (1982), 'To Know the Dancer from the Dance: Dance as a Metaphor
    of Marriage in Four Novels of Jane Austen', *Studies in the Novel*, 14 (1): 55–65.

Dredge, S. (2020), '"Was There a Servant … Who Did Not Know the Whole Story
    before the End of the Day?": Upside-down Points of View in Austen', *Persuasions
    Online*, 40 (2).

Dyde, B. (2000), *A History of Antigua: The Unsuspected Isle*, London: Macmillan.

Edmonds, A. (2013), *Jane Austen's Worthing: The Real Sanditon*, Stroud: Amberley.

Ferguson, M. (1991), '*Mansfield Park*: Slavery, Colonialism, and Gender', *Oxford Literary Review*, 13 (1/2): 118–39.

Freedgood, E. (2000), *Victorian Writing about Risk: Imagining a Safe England in a Dangerous World*, Cambridge: Cambridge University Press.

Freud, S. ([1901] 2002), *The Psychopathology of Everyday Life*, trans. A. Bell, Harmondsworth: Penguin.

Gay, P. (2002), *Jane Austen and the Theatre*, Cambridge: Cambridge University Press.

Girard, R. (1966), *Deceit, Desire and the Novel: Self and Other in Literary Structure*, trans. Y. Freccero, Baltimore, MD: The Johns Hopkins University Press.

Gorman, A. G. (1993), *The Body in Illness and Health: Themes and Images in Jane Austen*, New York, NY: Lang.

Halsey, K. (2006), 'The Blush of Modesty or the Blush of Shame? Reading Jane Austen's Blushes', *Forum for Modern Language Studies*, 42 (3): 226–38.

Hamilton, R. (2008), *Accident: A Philosophical and Literary History*, Chicago, IL: University of Chicago Press.

Hamrick, W. S. (2002), *Kindness and the Good Society: Connections of the Heart*, Albany, NY: State University of New York Press.

Harris, J. (2007), *A Revolution Almost beyond Expression: Jane Austen's 'Persuasion'*, Newark, DE: University of Delaware Press.

Harvey, W. J. (1967), 'The Plot of *Emma*', *Essays in Criticism*, 17 (1): 48–63.

Heydt-Stevenson, J. (2005), *Austen's Unbecoming Conjunctions: Subversive Laughter, Embodied History*, New York, NY: Palgrave.

Honan, P. (1987), *Jane Austen: Her Life*, New York, NY: Fawcett Columbine.

Hoydis, J. (2019), *Risk and the English Novel: From Defoe to McEwan*, Berlin: De Gruyter.

James, H. ([1905] 1984), 'The Lesson of Balzac', in L. Edel (ed.), *Literary Criticism Volume Two: European Writers and the Prefaces*, 115–39, New York, NY: Library of America.

Johnson, C. L. (2012), *Jane Austen's Cults and Cultures*, Chicago, IL: University of Chicago Press.

Johnston, F. (2021), *Jane Austen, Early and Late*, Princeton, NJ: Princeton University Press.

Kipling, R. (1926), 'The Janeites', in *Debits and Credits*, 147–76, London: Macmillan.

Lane, M. (2002), *Jane Austen and Names*, Bristol: Blaise.

Le Faye, D. (2004), *Jane Austen: A Family Record*, Cambridge: Cambridge University Press.

Lee, H. (2007), 'Jane Austen Faints', in *Virginia Woolf's Nose: Essays on Biography*, 63–94, Princeton, NJ: Princeton University Press.

Litvak, J. (1992), *Caught in the Act: Theatricality in the Nineteenth-Century English Novel*, Berkeley, CA: University of California Press.

Looser, D. (2017), *The Making of Jane Austen*, Baltimore, MA: The Johns Hopkins University Press.

Looser, D. (2021), 'Breaking the Silence', *TLS*, 21 May: 3.

Works Cited

Lynch, D., ed. (2000), *Janeites: Austen's Disciples and Devotees*, Princeton, NJ: Princeton University Press.

Malone, M. (2016), 'Jane Austen's Balls: *Emma*'s Dance of Masculinity', *Nineteenth-Century Literature*, 70 (4): 427–47.

Mansell, D. (1973), *The Novels of Jane Austen: An Interpretation*, London: Macmillan.

Markovits, S. (2007), 'Jane Austen and the Happy Fall', *Studies in English Literature, 1500–1900*, 47 (4): 779–97.

McMaster, J. (1995), *Jane Austen the Novelist: Essays Past and Present*, Basingstoke: Palgrave.

Miller, C. (2015), *Surprise: The Poetics of the Unexpected from Milton to Austen*, Ithaca, NY: Cornell University Press.

Miller, D. A. (1995), 'Austen's Attitude', *The Yale Journal of Criticism*, 8 (1): 1–5.

Miller, D. A. (2003), *Jane Austen, or The Secret of Style*, Princeton, NJ: Princeton University Press.

Mullan, J. (2012), *What Matters in Jane Austen? Twenty Crucial Puzzles Solved*, London: Bloomsbury.

O'Farrell, M. A. (1997), *Telling Complexions: The Nineteenth-Century English Novel and the Blush*, Durham, NC: Duke University Press.

Perry, R. (1986), 'Interrupted Friendships in Jane Austen's *Emma*', *Tulsa Studies in Women's Literature*, 5 (2): 185–202.

Phillips, A. (1994), 'Looking at Obstacles', in *On Kissing, Tickling, and Being Bored: Psychoanalytic Essays on the Unexamined Life*, 79–92, Cambridge, MA: Harvard University Press.

Porter, R. (1982), *English Society in the Eighteenth Century*, Harmondsworth: Penguin.

Potter, T. F. (1994), '"A Low but Very Feeling Tone": The Lesbian Continuum and Power Relations in Jane Austen's *Emma*', *ESC: English Studies in Canada*, 20 (2): 187–203.

Raff, S. (2014), *Jane Austen's Erotic Advice*, Oxford: Oxford University Press.

Ricks, C. (1996), 'Jane Austen and the Business of Mothering', in *Essays in Appreciation*, 90–113, Oxford: Clarendon Press.

Said, E. W. (1994), *Culture and Imperialism*, London: Vintage.

Salih, Sara (2006), 'The Silence of Miss Lambe: *Sanditon* and Contextual Fictions of "Race" in the Abolition Era', *Eighteenth-Century Fiction*, 18 (3): 329–53.

Sedgwick, E. K. (1991), 'Jane Austen and the Masturbating Girl', *Critical Inquiry*, 17 (4): 818–37.

Selwyn, D. (1998), *Jane Austen and Leisure*, London: Hambledon.

Selwyn, D. (2010), *Jane Austen and Children*, London: Continuum.

Spampinato, E. A. (2019), 'Tom Became What He Ought to Be: *Mansfield Park* as Homosocial Bildungsroman', *Studies in the Novel*, 51 (4): 481–98.

Stovel, B. (1989), 'Secrets, Silence, and Surprise in *Pride and Prejudice*', *Persuasions*, 11: 85–91.

Sulloway, A. G. (1989), *Jane Austen and the Province of Womanhood*, Philadelphia, PA: University of Pennsylvania Press.

Sutherland, K. (2017), 'Cents and Sensibility: Jane Austen's World of Risk', *Financial Times*, 16 June.

Tanner, T. (2007), *Jane Austen*, London: Palgrave.

Tave, S. (1973), *Some Words of Jane Austen*, Chicago, IL: University of Chicago Press.

Terry, J. (1988), 'Seen but Not Heard: Servants in Jane Austen's England', *Persuasions*, 10: 104–16.

Thomason, L. E. (2015), 'The Dilemma of Friendship in Austen's *Emma*', *The Eighteenth Century*, 56 (2): 227–41.

Tuite, C. (2002), *Romantic Austen: Sexual Politics and the Literary Canon*, Cambridge: Cambridge University Press.

Van Ostade, I. T-B. (2014), *In Search of Jane Austen: The Language of the Letters*, Oxford: Oxford University Press.

Walshe, N. (2014), 'The Importance of Servants in Jane Austen's Novels', *Persuasions Online*, 35 (1).

Watson, N. J. (1994), *Revolution and the Form of the British Novel, 1790–1825: Intercepted Letters, Interrupted Seductions*, Oxford: Clarendon Press.

Wheeler, D. (1998), 'The British Postal Service, Privacy, and Jane Austen's *Emma*', *South Atlantic Review*, 63 (4): 34–47.

Wheeler, D. (2003), 'Jane Austen and the Discourse of Poverty', *The Eighteenth-Century Novel*, 3: 243–62.

Williams, R. (1970), *The English Novel from Dickens to Lawrence*, London: Chatto.

Wiltshire, J. (1992), *Jane Austen and the Body: 'The Picture of Health'*, Cambridge: Cambridge University Press.

Wiltshire, J. (2003), 'Decolonising *Mansfield Park*', *Essays in Criticism*, 53 (4): 303–22.

Wiltshire, J. (2014), *The Hidden Jane Austen*, Cambridge: Cambridge University Press.

Woloch, A. (2003), *The One vs. the Many: Minor Characters and the Space of the Protagonist in the Novel*, Princeton, NJ: Princeton University Press.

Zionkowski, L. (2016), *Women and Gift Exchange in Eighteenth-Century Fiction: Richardson, Burney, Austen*, New York, NY: Routledge.

INDEX